Further stories for reading comprehension A

L A Hill

D1618896

Longman

INTRODUCTION

Further Stories for Reading Comprehension A and *B* follow on my *Stories for Reading Comprehension, Books 1, 2, and 3. Book A* follows the vocabulary and structure grading of the Longman Structural Readers up to and including Stage 5, and *Book B* takes the student up to Stage 6. A few words and structures outside the grading occur in each story, and these are listed on the inside back cover of the book, so that students and teachers can, if they wish, study them before using the book.

Each book consists of 20 stories divided up into groups of four. The first three stories in each group are funny, the fourth is serious.

After each story there are three exercises. The first exercise is purely a test of reading comprehension, and consists of questions with multiple choice answers. However, if the teacher wishes, he/she can read the story out to the students with their books shut and then ask the questions orally, thus using the story for aural comprehension.

The *Further Stories for Reading Comprehension* series has a new element; practice in composition. The second exercise in each unit aims to give the student practice in both comprehension and composition using alternate guided summary and vocabulary development exercises.

Finally, the third exercise gives the student guidance on a point of English structure using a grammar box, and then a test on her/his ability to use this structure.

In the middle of the book is a key which can be pulled out and distributed to the class after it has done an exercise. This allows for the maximum of time-saving for the teacher. The key also makes the books suitable for self-study.

Mary was seven years old. Her parents had recently moved to a new town, and so Mary was going to a different school from the one she had been at for some years. It was a few kilometres from the house which she now lived in with her parents, but there was a school bus that went around picking up pupils every morning and bringing them back to their homes every afternoon, and as both of Mary's parents had to go to work every morning, she always went on this bus. She had to be at a corner twenty metres from her front door by half past eight every day and the bus was usually on time, and never more than a minute or two late.

Mary's parents always set their alarm clock every evening so that none of them would be late, but one morning the alarm failed to go off, and it was not till a quarter past eight that Mary's mother suddenly woke up, looked at the clock, said, 'What ever's happened to that clock?' and then hurried into Mary's room. Mary was fast asleep, but her mother woke her up and told her to get ready for school.

'I'm sorry, dear,' she said, 'but you'll have to wash and dress very quickly, have an even quicker breakfast, and then I'll drive you to school on my way to the office. I'll get your breakfast ready now.'

'But how ever will you find the way, Mum?' Mary said. 'You've only been to school once.'

'Yes,' her mother answered, 'but you've done the trip several times now in the bus, so you can be my guide to get there, can't you?'

3

'Oh, yes,' said Mary, 'I suppose so.' She washed, dressed and had a quick breakfast, and then she and her mother went to the garage and got into the car.

They set off, and Mary told her mother to turn each time that they came to a place she recognised. In this way she made her mother drive round most of the town before they got to her school. When they arrived, her mother saw that it was not really very far from their house.

'Why ever did you make me go such a long way round, Mary, instead of the most direct way?' her mother asked her.

'Well, Mum,' answered Mary, 'it was because I didn't know how else to get here. That's the way our bus always goes to pick up the other children on the way to school.'

Exercise 1

Look at these questions. Find the right answers. Then write the questions and the answers:

1 Did Mary change schools?
   a) No, she did not.   b) Yes, she did.
2 Why did she do this?
   a) Because her parents went to another town.   b) Because she had been at the first school for some years.
3 Did Mary usually go to school in her mother's car?
   a) No, she did not.   b) Yes, she did.
4 Why was Mary late one morning?
   a) Because her mother's alarm clock did not go off.
   b) Because she was fast asleep.
5 Did Mary get her breakfast ready?
   a) No, she did not.   b) Yes, she did.
6 Did Mary know the way to school?
   a) No, she did not.   b) Yes, she did.
7 How did she know where her mother should turn?
   a) She was a guide.   b) She recognised each place.
8 Was the school really rather near, or a long way from, Mary's house?
   a) It was a long way from it.   b) It was rather near it.
9 Did Mary make her mother go a long way round?
   a) No, she did not.   b) Yes, she did.
10 Why did she do this?
   a) Because it was the way their bus went.   b) Because she didn't really know the way.

Exercise 2

Guided summary. A new neighbour arrives and she has a daughter who is going to go to Mary's school. She asks you these questions about it, and you must answer:

1 'How far away is the school?'
2 'How can pupils get there?'
3 'And how do they come home?'
4 'How far away is the place where Mary can get the bus?'
5 'At what time does she have to be there?'
6 'Is the bus punctual?'

The neighbour asks you these questions on the evening of the day the above story tells us about, and you must answer:

7 'Why wasn't Mary on the bus this morning?'
8 'How did she get to school?'
9 'Did her mother know the way'?
10 'How did she manage to get there?'
11 'What did she say when she got there?'
12 'And what did Mary answer?'

Exercise 3

> *Ever* can be put after *how, what, when, where, who(m)* or *why* to show that one is surprised, and sometimes also rather angry (e.g. 'Mary's parents found good new jobs.' 'How ever did they do that?' 'Mary missed the bus one afternoon.' 'What ever did she do that for?').

Ask these questions in a surprised way, using the words *in italics* and an expression with *ever*:

1 'Mary's parents moved to a new town.' '*Why* . . .?'
2 'Mary's mother did not wake until late.' '*How* . . . *happen*?'
3 'Mary's mother had an unusual car.' '*Where* . . . *find* . . .?'
4 'Mary made her mother go a long way before they reached her school.' '*What* . . . *for*?'
5 'Mary's mother played a lot of tennis.' '*When* . . . *find time* . . .?'
6 'Someone told Mary that soon there were not going to be any more school buses.' '*Who* . . . *told* . . .?'

Sally had been studying at an art college for a year and, like most students, she did not have much money. It was going to be her mother's birthday soon, and she wondered what she could buy her as a present that would be nice and useful but not too expensive.

Sally's college was in London, but she had been living in the country for many years, so every day she had an hour's journey by train in the morning, and the same in the evening.

At lunch time one day, a week before her mother's birthday, she decided to have a quick sandwich and a cup of coffee instead of her usual meal in the college hall, and then go shopping near her college to try to find her mother a nice present. When she had been looking for half an hour, she came across a shop that was selling umbrellas cheap, and decided that one of those would solve her problem, since her mother had lost hers the month before.

'Now which colour shall I choose?' she thought. 'Well, I think a black one would be the most useful really. You can carry that when you are wearing clothes of any colour, can't you?' So having made up her mind, she bought a lovely black umbrella and took it back to the college with her until her classes had finished.

On her way back home in the train that evening she felt hungry because she had had such a small lunch, so she went along to the buffet car for another sandwich and cup of coffee. She had left the black umbrella above her seat in the compartment, but when she got back, it had gone! When she had left the compartment, there had been no other passengers in it, but now there were three.

Sally burst into tears when she saw that the umbrella was no longer there. The other passengers felt very sorry for her and asked what the matter was. When she explained that the black umbrella she had bought for her mother had disappeared, and that she had to get out at the next station, the three other passengers asked her for her mother's address, in order to be able to send the umbrella on to her in case someone had removed it by mistake and not on purpose, and brought it back after Sally had got out of the train.

The next week, Sally heard from her mother. Her letter said, 'Thank you very much for your lovely presents, but why did you send me three black umbrellas?'

Exercise 1

Look at these questions. Find the right answers. Then write the questions and the answers:

1 What did Sally want to buy?
   a) A present for her birthday.   b) A present for her mother's birthday.

2 Why did it have to be rather cheap?
   a) Because, like most students, she was not rich.
   b) Because then it would be nice and useful.

3 Why did she have to go to her college by train?
   a) Because she lived in London.   b) Because she lived in the country.

4 Did she usually have a quick sandwich and a cup of coffee for her lunch?
   a) No, she did not.   b) Yes, she did.

5   Why did she not have her usual lunch one day?
    a) Because she needed the money to buy an umbrella.
    b) Because she did not have time to have it.
6   Why did she choose a black umbrella?
    a) Because it was cheap.   b) Because it was suitable for
    wearing with any clothes.
7   Why did she leave the umbrella in her compartment in the
    train?
    a) Because she wanted to have a sandwich and a cup of
    coffee.   b) Because there were no other passengers there.
8   Was the umbrella there when she came back?
    a) No, it was not.   b) Yes, it was.
9   Why did the other passengers say they wanted Sally's
    mother's address?
    a) To send her another umbrella.   b) To send her the
    umbrella if it was brought back by someone.
10 Do you think that someone did bring the umbrella back
    to the compartment?
    a) No.   b) Yes.

Exercise 2

In each of these (pairs of) sentences fill the empty space with
a word that has the same root as the word *in italics*:

1   Sally was a *student*. She was . . . art.
2   She was studying *art* because she wanted to become an
    . . ..
3   Her *usual* lunch was a salad, but one day she did not go
    into the college hall as . . ., and had a sandwich and a cup
    of coffee instead.
4   She sometimes went to the *shops* at lunch time, but she
    also went . . . on Saturday mornings.
5   She did not want to buy a brightly *coloured* umbrella
    because her mother did not wear . . . clothes.
6   A black umbrella was *useful* to Sally's mother, but a
    brightly coloured one would have been . . . as she never
    wore bright clothes.
7   Sally had a *small* lunch. Because of the . . . of this
    lunch she was very hungry by five o'clock.
8   She burst into *tears* when she lost the umbrella, and
    answered the other passengers . . . when they asked her
    what the matter was.

9 She gave the other passengers her mother's *address*, and they . . . their parcels to her.
10 You can see from a person's date of *birth* when her or his . . . will be.

Exercise 3

The *had been doing* tense is used to show that an action in the past happened before something else and continued without a break for some time (e.g. Sally was tired at five o'clock because she had been working hard since lunch time). The *had done* tense is usually used to show that the action happened before something else (e.g. When Sally had finished her work, she went home).

Copy these sentences, putting the verbs in brackets into the *had been doing* or the *had done* tense:

1 Sally (study) art for one year when this story began.
2 She went out shopping when she (finish) her morning's work.
3 She had to send the umbrella to her mother instead of taking it to her because she (live) away from home for two years.
4 When she (buy) the umbrella she took it back to her college.
5 She found that the umbrella (go) when she returned from the buffet car.
6 The other passengers in the compartment (sit) there since the train left the last station.
7 They (read) their evening papers for all that time.
8 When Sally told them that she (lose) an umbrella, they were very sorry.

UNIT

3

Mrs Grey lived in the country, but she worked in London, the capital of England. She always drove to the railway station in her car every morning, and left it in the station car park until she arrived back in the train in the evening. She was a careful driver, but one morning she was rather late, so she was going rather faster than usual when she had an accident in a narrow road not far from her home.

What happened was that another car was coming in the opposite direction, and either that one or Mrs Grey's car was too far in the middle of the road, or perhaps both of them were. They ran into each other and were both damaged, although not enough to stop them being driven.

Both Mrs Grey and the other driver, who was a young man whom she had seen in the district but had not met, got out of their cars, and Mrs Grey said, 'I'm afraid I haven't got time to waste on an accident this morning, as I have a very important appointment in town at nine, and I suppose you're a busy man too.'

'Yes, I am,' the young man said, 'but we'll have to call the police for insurance purposes, won't we? They won't pay for the damage unless we have reported the accident to the police and they have come and seen what happened.'

'Yes, certainly,' Mrs Grey answered, 'but I have something to suggest. We won't be committing a crime if we go away now in our cars, and then come back to the scene of the accident, say, at six this evening, and put them in exactly the same positions as they are in now. Then we can call the police. They won't know what time the accident happened, and the insurance companies won't care either as long as we can send them a police report of the accident.'

'What a good idea!' the young man said happily. 'So I'll be waiting here at six o'clock this evening. I won't be late!'

'Nor will I,' Mrs Grey answered. She and the young man exchanged visiting cards, and then each drove off to carry on with their work.

When Mrs Grey arrived at the station from London at a quarter to six that evening, she got into her car, drove to the place where the accident had happened, and found the young man waiting there in his car. They put both cars in exactly the same positions as they had been in after the accident, and then Mrs Grey called the police, using the telephone in her car, as if the accident had just happened.

Exercise 1

Look at these questions. Find the right answers. Then write the questions and the answers:

1 How did Mrs Grey get to London every morning?
   a) By car.   b) By car and train.   c) By train.
2 Why did she have an accident one morning?
   a) Because she was going fast.   b) Because she was on a narrower road than usual.
3 Were the cars so badly damaged that they could not be driven away?
   a) No, they were not.   b) Yes, they were.
4 Did Mrs Grey know the driver of the other car?
   a) Only by sight.   b) Yes, because she had talked to him.
5 Why did Mrs Grey not want to call the police at once?
   a) Because she was too busy.   b) Because the accident had been her fault.
6 Why was it necessary to call the police?
   a) So that they could pay for the damage.   b) To get money from their insurance companies.
7 What did Mrs Grey plan to do?
   a) To commit a crime.   b) To meet the young man in the same place that evening.
8 How did they know each other's name?
   a) They exchanged visiting cards.   b) They told each other their names.
9 Who arrived first at the place where the accident had happened?
   a) Mrs Grey.   b) The young man.

10 How did they get the police to come?
   a) Mrs Grey called a policeman who was passing.
   b) Mrs Grey phoned them from her car.

Exercise 2

Guided summary. Complete this paragraph, using what you have read in the above story:

A few mornings ago Helen drove to the station as usual. She had never had an accident, because . . ., but that morning she was going rather fast, because . . ., and she ran into . . .. She did not have time . . ., because she had . . .. The other man . . . too, so they agreed to . . .. When Helen got back to the station that evening, she drove . . .. The young man . . .. They put their cars . . . and then Helen used . . . to call . . ..

Exercise 3

The *will do* tense is used to show that an action is going to happen in the future (e.g. Mrs Grey will start work at nine). The *will be doing* tense can be used to show that the action will not yet have finished at a certain time in the future (e.g. At five o'clock, Mrs Grey will still be working).

Copy these sentences, putting the verbs in brackets into the *will do* or *will be doing* tense:

1 Mrs Grey said, 'I can't see you at ten, because I (work) then. I start at nine.'
2 Then she said, 'I (finish) at twelve, so I (see) you then.'
3 The young man said, 'I (drive) here from the station at six, and I (wait) here when you arrive at half past six.'
4 Mrs Grey lives in the country, and she expects she (still live) there when the time comes for her to retire.
5 Mrs Grey said, 'Don't come to see me next Sunday, because I (stay) with my sister in Southampton then.'
6 Mrs Grey (not finish) lunch till one, so don't phone her at half past twelve; she (still eat) then.

4

In many countries now seat belts are compulsory for the driver and front seat passenger at least.

Most doctors believe that seat belts save people from being seriously hurt in a crash, but there are some people who still think that it is more dangerous to wear a seat belt than not to wear one.

They say that a seat belt may trap one in a car that is burning, or that has fallen into a river or the sea and is sinking, so that one is burnt to death or drowned.

But less than half of one per cent of car accidents lead to fire or sinking, and in any case, a seat belt may easily save a person from being knocked unconscious in an accident, so that he or she is able to undo the seat belt immediately and get out of a car that is on fire or sinking.

People who object to seat belts also sometimes say that without one, one may be thrown right out of a car in a crash, but doctors will tell you that that is the last thing one wants to happen: if one is thrown out of a car, one hits something, usually the road, and usually hard and at speed. It is better to remain inside a car in the case of a crash.

There is also the question of personal freedom; some people say that it is an attack on their freedom to force them to wear a seat belt, whether they want to or not. But even in a democracy there are a lot of things a person is denied the right to do though he or she wants to do them. I may, for example, want to play music loudly all night; it interferes with my freedom if I am not allowed to do this. But my neighbours have their own rights to freedom, just as I have. They want to be free to sleep quietly at night, and if I stop them doing so, I am interfering with their freedom.

How does this affect seat belts? In what way does it interfere with the rights of others if someone refuses to wear a seat belt? Well, first of all because common sense tells us that a driver without a seat belt has less control of a car if there is an accident, so that he or she is more likely to be a danger to others, who after all also have the right to be protected as much as possible from accident.

But also there is the question of the cost of being hurt. A driver expects to be taken to hospital free of charge by ambulance if he or she is hurt in a crash. He or she also expects to be looked after properly in hospital, again free of charge. Who pays for this? In most countries the people who pay the taxes do so. And they have a right to demand that the amount they pay should be kept as low as possible by making sure that people do not hurt themselves unnecessarily by not taking proper care such as wearing a seat belt.

Exercise 1

Look at these questions. Find the right answers. Then write the questions and the answers:

1 Do all people believe that seat belts are a good thing?
    a) No, they do not.   b) Yes, they do.
2 Why do some people say that they are dangerous?
    a) Because they may make a car burn or fall into a river.
    b) Because they may prevent one escaping from a burning or sinking car.
3 Do a lot of cars catch fire or fall into deep water?
    a) No.   b) Yes.
4 How can a seat belt help if one's car does catch fire or sink?
    a) It can knock one unconscious, so that one does not feel anything.   b) It can stop one from being knocked unconscious, so that one can escape.
5 Do doctors say that it is better or worse to be thrown out of a car if it has an accident?
    a) They say it is better.   b) They say it is worse.

6 Why?
   a) Because if one is thrown out of a car one is not hurt.
   b) Because if one is thrown out of a car one is hurt.
7 Are we free to do what we want in a democracy?
   a) No, we are not.   b) Yes, we are.
8 What limits our freedom?
   a) Nothing.   b) The rights of others.
9 Why may our not wearing a seat belt affect other people?
   a) Because it may cause us to lose control of the car and
   hit theirs.   b) Because then they may refuse to wear seat
   belts too.
10 How does not wearing seat belts affect people who pay
   taxes?
   a) It leads to more ambulance and hospital costs.   b) It
   means that they get more things free of charge.

Exercise 2

In each of these (pairs of) sentences, fill the empty space with
a word that has the same root as the word *in italics*:

1 A lot of people are *seriously* hurt in car crashes, but one
   often cannot tell the . . . of the damage done to them until
   they get to hospital.
2 One passenger was *dead* when the police found him. He
   had been burnt to . . . .
3 One can say, 'She was killed in an *accident*', or 'She was
   killed . . . .'
4 A blow with plenty of *force* can be called a . . . blow.
5 People who do not wear seat belts are in *danger*, and I for
   one do not like living . . . .
6 A *person* who wants . . . freedom for herself or himself but
   not for others is a selfish person.
7 We all want to be *free*, but we cannot have this . . . when
   it hurts others.
8 It is foolish to *refuse* to wear a seat belt if this . . . costs
   others a lot of money.
9 Common *sense* will tell any . . . person that a driver
   without a seat belt has less control of a car.
10 A bus *crashed* on a bridge last week, and a lot of people
   were hurt in the . . . .

Exercise 3

> Someone *may do* something can mean 'it is possible that someone does (or will do) something' (e.g. An ambulance is coming, but it may be late because of the fog). Someone *may have done* something can mean 'it is possible that someone did (or has done) something' (e.g. The doctor is late; he may have been slowed down by the fog).

Write these sentences, putting the verbs in brackets in the correct form, using *may*:

1 Passengers in the front seats have to wear seat belts, and soon ones in the back seats (have) to wear them too.
2 There is a car in the sea there! It (fall) down that cliff.
3 There is also a man in the sea. He is swimming to the shore. He (be) in the car.
4 He (swim) to us when he sees us.
5 He (owe) his life to his seat belt.
6 There (be) passengers in the back seat of the car too when it fell down the cliff.
7 The fall (knock) them unconscious and they (be) in the car still.
8 That boat (save) them.

5

Sarah had a son of ten, who was called Jack. He did not like studying, but loved watching television. Sarah used to drive to school at half past four in the afternoon, bring Jack back home and give him his tea, but as soon as he got into the house, he always rushed to the television set and turned it on.

'Haven't you got any homework, Jack?' his mother always asked him as she began to make the tea.

'Eh? Oh, yes, I've got a little,' he used to answer. 'I'll do it later when there's nothing interesting on television.'

At first Sarah had allowed Jack to watch television instead of starting on his homework first, but she soon discovered that he never had a *little* homework – it was always a great deal – and that there was never a time when there was nothing interesting on television, so that after putting off doing his homework for a couple of hours, Jack was too tired to do his homework properly, if at all.

Sarah then decided to make him do it first. This was always a battle, and often when Jack obeyed his mother, he did the work quickly and carelessly in order to finish it and get back to his beloved television.

The result was the same as when he left his homework until last; bad work, which he was punished for the next day at school by getting low marks, either because his homework was full of mistakes, or because he did not know the work he was supposed to have prepared the night before.

One evening Jack's science homework was about famous inventors like Thomas Edison, who made important discoveries and inventions in the field of electricity. When he had homework that consisted of learning facts, his mother had begun to test him when he finished, to try to make sure that he had really done the work properly and not left anything out, and this is what she did this time. She did not let him stop until she was sure that he knew what was in his book.

But this time, it was less of a battle than usual to make Jack sit down and go over what he had to learn carefully, because it had a strong connection with television.

In class the next day, the teacher said to Jack, 'What are some of the things that Thomas Edison did for science?'

'Well,' Jack answered happily, 'first of all, if it weren't for Edison, we'd all be watching television by candlelight!'

Exercise 1

Look at these questions. Find the right answers. Then write the questions and the answers:

1 Did Jack have homework?
   a) No, he did not.   b) Yes, he had a little.   c) Yes, he had a lot.
2 Why did he not do it well?
   a) Because he was not a clever boy.   b) Because he was too interested in television.
3 When did he say he would do it?
   a) When his mother made the tea.   b) When there was nothing interesting on television.
4 Was there sometimes nothing interesting on television for Jack?
   a) No, there was not.   b) Yes, there was.
5 What happened after a couple of hours?
   a) Jack did his homework badly, or he did not do it at all.
   b) Jack put off doing his homework.
6 What did Jack's mother do then?
   a) She beat him.   b) She forced him to do his homework before he watched television.
7 Did this produce good results?
   a) No, because Jack did not do his homework at all.
   b) No, because Jack did not do his homework well.
   c) Yes, it did.
8 What did Jack's mother do then to stop him being punished at school?
   a) She began to test him after he had done his homework.
   b) She gave him low marks.

9   Why did Jack enjoy doing his homework about Thomas Edison?
    a) Because his mother let him sit down.   b) Because it had something to do with television.

10 If there was no electricity, could we watch television by candelight?
    a) No, we could not.   b) Yes, we could.

Exercise 2

Guided summary. Write a summary of the above story by answering these questions. Do not use numbers:

1   Who was Jack? (*Jack was* . . .)
2   How much homework did he always have? Why did he delay doing it every day? (. . . *but* . . .)
3   What did his mother let him do at first?
4   What was the result?
5   What did his mother do then?
6   What was the result?
7   What did his mother begin to do then?
8   Why was this less difficult than usual one day?
9   What did the teacher ask Jack the next day? (*The next day the teacher asked him what* . . .)
10 And what did Jack answer? (*and Jack answered that* . . .)

Exercise 3

It is possible to turn a verb (phrase) into the object of certain other verbs by putting it into the -*ing* form (e.g. instead of 'Sarah reads a lot; she likes it' we can say 'Sarah likes reading' and instead of 'Jack watches a lot of television; he enjoys it' we can say 'Jack enjoys watching television').

Change these sentences, replacing *it* by an -*ing* form of the verb and the rest of the phrase, if there is one. Start each sentence with the words in brackets:

1   Most children watch television. They begin *it* when they are very young, and continue *it* all their lives. (Most children begin . . .)

2 Other children play games instead, because they enjoy *it*. (Other children enjoy . . .)

3 Some adults want to make children do their homework instead. They try *it*, and sometimes they are successful. (Some adults try . . .)

4 Some children do a lot of homework, and they do not seem to mind *it*. (Some children do not seem to mind . . .)

5 Other children watch television. They prefer *it*. (Other children prefer . . .)

6 We had no television when I was a child. I remember *it*. (I remember not . . .)

7 I wrote my own stories and drew pictures for them. I shall never forget *it*. (I shall never forget . . .)

8 I still do this. I shall never stop *it*. (I shall never stop . . .)

6

Alan Brown liked the novels of a writer whose name was Fraser Lambourn very much, and as Alan's wife Violet was the manager of a big bookshop, she always brought Alan back the latest work by his favourite writer.

Then one day Violet said to her husband, 'Guess what, Alan! Fraser Lambourn's coming to our bookshop next week to sign copies of his new book for people who buy it! Isn't that good news?'

'Yes, it's wonderful!' said Alan happily. Then he stopped and thought for a few seconds. 'But you've already brought me a copy of his new book!' he said disappointedly. 'I don't suppose he'll sign that, will he?'

'Oh, yes, he will,' said Violet cheerfully. 'You just wait and see.' She told Alan that her bookshop was giving Fraser Lambourn a party at the Grand Hotel before he started signing, and that he would owe her something for that. 'You've been invited as my husband, by the way,' Violet added, 'so you can have a word with him there.' Alan became happy again, and he eagerly looked forward to the Saturday on which he would meet Fraser Lambourn.

The day came at last, and at the time Violet had told him, Alan was at the door of the hotel room where the party was going to be, looking inside to see if he could recognise his favourite writer, whose photograph he had had for a long time. He had a small black beard.

'Yes, there he is!' he said to himself excitedly. 'And he's having a conversation with Violet! Hurrah! What luck!' He went in, and said, 'Hullo, dear' to his wife. She introduced him to the great man.

'Mr Lambourn . . .,' Violet began.

'Oh, do please call me Fraser,' the writer interrupted with a smile.

'Thank you, Fraser,' Violet said. Then she turned to Alan and said, 'Fraser was telling me about his early days as a writer. It was most interesting. Could you repeat what you were saying for Alan, Fraser?'

'Certainly,' Fraser answered. 'I was telling your charming wife that my real name was Larry Lamb, but that my agent had advised me to change it if I wanted to find a publisher. How right he was!'

'And you were telling me something else too, Fraser,' said Violet with a smile.

'Oh, yes,' the writer continued, 'I was telling Violet that it wasn't till I'd been writing for twelve years that I discovered I had no talent at all as a writer.'

Alan was very surprised and asked Fraser why he hadn't given up writing then.

'I couldn't,' declared Fraser. 'By that time I was too famous to stop.'

Exercise 1

Look at these questions. Find the right answers. Then write the questions and the answers:

1   How did Alan get Fraser Lambourn's books?
    a) He bought them at a big bookshop.   b) His wife brought them to him.
2   What did Alan hope to do when Fraser came to the bookshop?
    a) He hoped to buy a copy of his new book.   b) He hoped to get him to sign a copy of his new book.
3   Why did Alan think Fraser would not do this?
    a) Because he did not have a copy of the book.
    b) Because Violet had already brought him the book.

4 Why was Violet sure that Fraser would sign Alan's copy of the book?
a) Because he owed her some money. b) Because the bookshop was having a party for him.

5 How did Alan recognise Fraser?
a) Because he had a beard. b) Because he had a photograph of him.

6 Why was Alan lucky when he went into the hotel room?
a) Because Fraser was talking to Violet. b) Because Violet introduced him to Fraser.

7 What was the writer's real name?
a) Fraser Lambourn. b) Larry Lamb.

8 Did he change it?
a) No, he did not. b) Yes, he did.

9 What did Fraser find out after twelve years?
a) That he was getting very little money as a writer.
b) That he was not at all a good writer.

10 Did he stop writing then?
a) No, he did not. b) Yes, he did.

Exercise 2

In each of these (pairs of) sentences fill the empty space with a word that has the same root as the word *in italics*:

1 A person who *writes* books can be called a . . . .

2 A person who writes *novels* can also be called a . . . .

3 Alan was very *disappointed* when he thought Fraser would not sign his book, but his . . . did not last long.

4 'Did you *invite* Fraser Lambourn to a party?' 'Yes, I sent him an . . . last month.'

5 Alan was *eagerly* looking forward to meeting Fraser, and in his . . . he arrived at the hotel an hour early.

6 The *photograph* of Fraser that Alan had had been taken by a famous London . . ..

7 Alan was very *excited* when he saw Fraser talking to Violet, and in his . . . he caught his foot on a carpet and fell.

8 'What *luck*!' he thought when he saw Violet with the great man. 'This is really my . . . day!'

9 Everything about Fraser *interested* Alan. He thought he was the most . . . writer he had ever known.

10 When Fraser's agent *advised* him to change his name, he followed his . . ..

Exercise 3

When the verb that introduces indirect speech is in a past tense (e.g. *said, had said*) the verbs in the direct speech are changed so that present tenses become past, and past tenses become past perfect (e.g. 'Violet said, "Alan is reading a novel"' becomes 'Violet said that Alan was reading a novel' and 'Alan said, "I met Fraser at a party"' becomes 'Alan said that he had met Fraser at a party').

Change these sentences into indirect speech:

1 Violet said to Alan, 'Fraser Lambourn's coming to the bookshop soon, and he's going to sign copies of his new book.'
2 Alan said to Violet, 'You've already brought me a copy of his new book.'
3 Violet said, 'Fraser was telling me about his early days as a writer, and it was most interesting.'
4 Fraser said, 'My real name is Larry Lamb, but my agent advised me to change it.'
5 Alan said to a friend, 'My wife works in a bookshop.'

Joan was very good at science when she was at school, and she was especially interested in computers, so when she finished her education she decided to work with them.

She very much enjoyed the work in the office she joined, and soon she was able to do unusually clever things with computers.

'They're really like friends to me nowadays,' Joan told her mother one evening during supper. 'I can ask them questions, and they answer just like people, but more politely and without arguing, and without one having to wonder whether one is going to hurt their feelings. And they never lie!'

'I should hope not!' her mother answered. 'It sounds like the perfect companion – or husband – doesn't it?' They both laughed. 'But can any of them think for themselves?'

'I'm afraid not,' Joan said. 'You can get no more out of them than what you've put in. It's called programming. But it's wonderful what you can get them to do.'

'Well,' Joan's mother said, 'I'm curious to know whether you can programme one of them to give me some advice.'

'I hope so,' answered Joan. 'I'll try it out. What do you want advice about?'

'Well,' her mother answered, 'you know my two watches, don't you?'

'Yes,' Joan answered doubtfully. 'What advice can a computer give you about them?'

'Well,' her mother answered, 'one of them gains one second every hour, and the other has stopped and won't start again. I'd be grateful to know which I should keep. Do you mind asking one of your computers?'

Joan laughed and answered, 'That's a strange thing to ask a computer, but I'll do so. I'll ask Donald. He's my best computer.'

When she got home the next evening, her mother had forgotten all about her request for advice.

'You remember what you asked about your two watches, Mum?' she said.

'Eh? What's that? My two watches? Oh, yes. I don't suppose your computer could give me any advice.'

'Oh, yes, he could!' Joan replied. 'Donald had the answer in a flash.'

'Donald?' said her mother. 'Oh, you mean your favourite computer.'

'Yes,' answered Joan. 'Donald advised you to keep the watch that has stopped.'

'The watch that has stopped?' Joan's mother said. 'Why ever did he advise that?'

'Because he pointed out that that watch will be right once every twelve hours, but the other one will be right only once every five years.'

Exercise 1

Look at these questions. Find the right answers. Then write the questions and the answers:

1 Why did Joan enjoy the work in her office?
   a) Because she had a lot of friends there.   b) Because she could work with computers there.
2 Why did Joan think computers were better than people?
   a) Because they were politer and never felt hurt.
   b) Because they never went to sleep.
3 What did Joan's mother think about computers?
   a) That her husband would like one as a perfect companion.   b) That they were like perfect husbands.
4 Could Joan's computers think for themselves?
   a) No, they could not.   b) Yes, they could.
5 How did Joan make her computers think?
   a) By getting more out of them than she put in.   b) By programming them.
6 What did Joan's mother want a computer to do?
   a) To advise her on which watch to buy.   b) To advise her on which watch to keep.
7 What was wrong with her first watch?
   a) It was fast.   b) It was slow.
8 And what was wrong with her other watch?
   a) It would not go.   b) It would not stop.

9   Which watch did the computer advise her to keep?
    a) The one that had stopped.   b) The one that was fast.
10 Was that useful advice for Joan's mother?
    a) No, it was not.   b) Yes, it was.

Exercise 2

Guided summary. You are Joan's friend and you want to write
a letter to your husband, who is working abroad.

Tell him:
how Joan likes her work.
how Joan's computers answer her questions.
what Joan's mother thought about Joan's computers.
what she wanted advice about from a computer.
what advice the computer gave her.
why it gave her this advice.

Exercise 3

> To avoid having to repeat the words that another person
> has said, one can sometimes use *so* or *not* (e.g. 'I think
> that computers are very useful.' 'I think so too'; this
> means 'I think that computers are very useful too.' 'Can
> you use a computer?' 'I'm afraid not'; this means 'I'm
> afraid I can't use a computer').

Copy these sentences, but replace the parts *in italics* by
so or *not*:

1   'Joan is very good at science.' 'Yes, it appears *that Joan is
    very good at science.*'
2   'There are few people who can programme computers
    well.' 'Yes, I suppose *there are few people who can programme
    computers well.*'
3   'Have you got a computer?' 'I am afraid *that I have not got
    a computer.*'
4   'I think Joan's mother's watches can be repaired.' 'I hope
    Joan's mother's watches can be repaired.'
5   'Did Joan's mother find Donald's advice useful?' 'I guess
    that she did not find his advice useful.'
6   'Joan's mother wants to get a computer now.' 'Who said
    that Joan's mother wants to get a computer now?'

For thousands of years people have been interested in comets. Why?

Often because they have been afraid of them; they have thought they were signs of terrible things to come, and they were afraid they might hit the earth. In fact, small pieces of comets do from time to time fall on our earth in the form of meteors, some of which are quite large pieces of solid material. One can see examples of these in some museums.

What is a comet? It is a body that goes round our sun, not in a circle like the planets, but in a kind of egg shape that takes it round our solar system, or in some cases perhaps even outside it, and then back in again. The nearest any comet gets to the edge of our sun during its orbits is about 145,000 kilometres. The shortest orbit is three years, and the longest is likely to be something like a million years. There are thought to be about 120,000 comets in our solar system.

A comet has a head and one or more long tails. What are they made of? Most scientists believe they are frozen gases and dust, but recently there has been another idea, which is that the head is made of organic material in one or more solid pieces.

How did the comets begin? We do not know, any more than we know how our solar system as a whole began.

Why are comets of scientific interest? Because it is likely that they have changed little if at all since they were first formed, so that they could give us interesting information about the beginnings of our solar system, including our earth. If they are made up of organic material, they could also give us valuable information about the beginnings of life on our earth, especially if, as some scientists now think, the small pieces that fall on our earth can lead to organic changes in it.

Two famous scientists have thought for some time that comets bring living things to earth which are the causes of diseases that have started suddenly among people and animals and that have not been able to be explained before. They say that recent discoveries made with very big telescopes and by the spacecraft Giotto have made this idea more likely to be true. But there are other scientists who do not agree. To get proof of who is right, it is likely that we shall have to wait until we have spacecraft that can get much closer to a comet than they have been able to do so far.

Exercise 1

Look at these questions. Find the right answers. Then write the questions and the answers:

1 What is one reason why people have been afraid of comets?
   a) Because they thought they meant that terrible things had happened.   b) Because they thought they meant that terrible things were going to happen.
2 What was another reason?
   a) That they saw examples of them in museums.
   b) That they thought a comet might fall on the earth.
3 How does a comet go round the sun?
   a) In a circle.   b) In an egg shape.
4 Do all comets stay inside our solar system?
   a) No.   b) We are not sure.   c) Yes.
5 Are there differences between the orbits of different comets?
   a) No, there are not.   b) Yes, there are small ones.
   c) Yes, there are very big ones.
6 What did scientists use to believe comets were made of?
   a) Dust and gases.   b) Organic material.
7 What could we find out from comets if they were made of dust and gases?
   a) How our own earth began.   b) How they have changed since they were first formed.

8 What may we perhaps find out from comets if they are made of organic material?
a) The beginnings of life on our earth.   b) The beginnings of our solar system.

9 What may have caused some diseases that have started suddenly on our earth?
a) Organic material from comets.   b) People and animals that have not been able to be explained before.

10 Have we got proof of these things yet?
a) No, we have not.   b) Yes, we have.

Exercise 2

In each of these (pairs of) sentences, fill the empty space with a word that has the same root as the word *in italics*:

1 We can say, 'Because some comets have a very *short* orbit, we see them quite often' or 'Because of the . . . of some comets' orbits, we see them quite often.'

2 *Science* has taught us a lot about comets. They are of great . . . interest to the . . . who study them all over the world.

3 It is possible to *freeze* gases and dust to try to copy the . . . material of which comets may be made.

4 People do not usually like *dust*, because they think that . . . places are dirty.

5 We can say, 'We know very little about how our solar system *began*' or 'We know very little about the . . . of our solar system.'

6 We can say, 'What is the *value* of such information?' or 'How . . . is such information?'

7 We have *discovered* quite a lot about comets recently, but there will be much more important . . . when we have better spacecraft.

8 Is it *true* that comets are made of organic matter? It is important to know the . . . about such matters.

9 At present scientists do not *agree* about the material of which comets are made. It would be good if some . . . could be reached soon.

10 We can say 'To get *proof* of who is right, we shall have to get much closer to a comet' or 'To . . . who is right we must get much closer to a comet.'

Exercise 3

> Instead of having a clause as the subject of a verb (e.g. That comets go round the sun is true), it is usual to use *it* as the subject, and then put the clause after the verb (e.g. It is true that comets go round the sun).
>
> Instead of having an indefinite subject (e.g. a noun with *a(n)*, *some* (/səm/), *any* etc.) with the verb *to be*, it is usual to have impersonal *there* (/ðeəʳ/) as the subject, and to put the noun with *a(n)* etc. after the verb (e.g. 'Some fog is between us and the comet' becomes 'There is some fog between us and the comet').

Put *it* or *there* in each space in these sentences:

1 ... is a fact that small pieces of comets fall on our earth; ... is no doubt about it.
2 ... is probable that ... are about 120,000 comets in our solar system.
3 ... are scientists who think that ... is organic pieces of comets that cause some diseases on our earth.
4 ... are not yet spacecraft that can get close enough to comets to see if ... is true that they are made of organic materials.

9

Mr and Mrs Jones were farmers. They had a small farm, on which they had worked very hard for ages, and they had five children. They had to look after their animals every day from sunrise to sunset, so they never had time for holidays.

But when Mrs Jones was sixty, and Mr Jones was sixty-five, they decided to let two of their children, who had stayed on on the farm after leaving school, run it for them for two weeks while they went off and had a holiday for the first time at the seaside.

They decided to go to Bournemouth in their old car, and to do some sightseeing in it if possible during their week by the sea. They booked a room in a nice hotel and studied maps to see where they would go for their sightseeing trips in the Bournemouth area.

They started out fairly early one Monday morning in the car, after milking the cows, and reached Bournemouth at eleven o'clock. There they stopped and asked a nice policeman who looked like their son the way to their hotel, and were soon registering at the desk there. Parking the car was no problem, because there was a car park just behind the hotel, and soon they were in a nice room from which they could see the sea and the beautiful sandy beach.

After they had unpacked their cases, they discussed what to do the rest of that day. The sun was shining brightly, and the sea was calm, so they thought they would go down on to the beach. There were already a lot of other people there, bathing, playing games or just lying in the sun.

'We can wait till tomorrow for our first trip,' Mrs Jones said. 'Let's go and see Salisbury then, shall we? We've always wanted to go there.'

'All right,' said her husband, 'that's a good idea.' They changed into suitable cool cotton clothes for a walk by the sea, but as they were about to leave the room to go downstairs, Mrs Jones saw a notice on the inside of the door of their room. It said, 'Breakfast 7.00–10.00. Lunch 11.30–2.30. Tea 3.00–5.30. Dinner 6.30–12.00.'

'Look at this, dear,' she said to her husband. He looked for a few seconds and then said in a disappointed voice, 'That doesn't allow us much time for sightseeing, does it?'

Exercise 1

Look at these questions. Find the right answers. Then write the questions and the answers:

1 Why had Mr and Mrs Jones not had time for a holiday before?
   a) Because they had animals to look after.   b) Because they had five children to look after their animals.
2 Why were they able to have a holiday at last?
   a) Because Mrs Jones was sixty, and Mr Jones was sixty-five.   b) Because they had two children to run the farm for them.
3 Did they plan to spend all their holiday in Bournemouth?
   a) No, they planned to do some sightseeing too.   b) No, they planned to study maps too.   c) Yes, they did.
4 Did they know the way to their hotel before they reached Bournemouth?
   a) No, they did not.   b) Yes, they did.
5 Who told them how to get there?
   a) A policeman did.   b) Their son did.
6 Where did they park their car?
   a) Just behind the hotel.   b) On a beautiful sandy beach.
7 When did they decide to visit Salisbury?
   a) That afternoon.   b) The next day.
8 Why did they go out of their room?
   a) To go to Salisbury.   b) To have a walk by the sea.
9 Why was Mr Jones disappointed when he saw the notice on their door?
   a) Because he did not like to have meals so late.
   b) Because he thought the times of meals left no time for sightseeing.
10 What mistake had he made?
   a) He had thought one could eat at any time between the times shown.   b) He had thought one had to eat meals during the whole time shown.

Exercise 2

Guided summary. Complete this paragraph, using what you have read in the above story:

I know Mrs Jones. She is a farmer, and so is . . . . They had never had a holiday because . . ., but then at last they were able to have one because . . . . They decided . . ., and they also wanted . . . . They chose places . . . by looking at . . . . They did not know . . ., so they asked . . . . They parked . . . . They decided not to . . . . As they were . . ., they saw . . . . It gave the times . . . . Mr Jones felt . . . because he thought . . ., but the mistake he made was . . . .

Exercise 3

So as not to have to repeat a noun, one can sometimes put *who, whom* or *that* instead. Use *who* and *whom* for people (e.g. 'Some of the people went into the sea; they got cold' can become 'The people who went into the sea got cold') and *that* for animals and things (e.g. 'Mr and Mrs Jones went to the hotel; it was the nearest to the sea' becomes 'Mr and Mrs Jones went to the hotel that was the nearest to the sea'). When *who(m)* or *that* is the object, it can be left out (e.g. 'They were looking at some people on the beach; they were bathing' becomes 'The people (who(m)) they were looking at on the beach were bathing' and 'They had a meal in a restaurant; it was good' becomes 'The meal (that) they had in a restaurant was good').

Join each pair of these sentences, using *who, whom* or *that* in place of the nouns or noun phrases *in italics*. Then copy your sentences again, leaving out *who, whom, that* if this is possible:

1 Mr and Mrs Jones had to look after the animals. *The animals* were on their farm.
2 The people were their children. *These people* looked after the farm when Mr and Mrs Jones were away.
3 The hotel was near the sea. Mr and Mrs Jones had chosen *the hotel*.
4 The people were bathing, playing games or just lying on the beach. Mr and Mrs Jones saw *these people*.

Read. Compr. (A)

- p 13-14   л 4
- p 10-11   л 3
- p. 35   w 10

10

Mrs Matthews lived in a small town where there was one jeweller's shop. It also took in watch repairs, although it had to send them off to London for the work to be done, as there was not enough business to keep an expert watch repairer occupied.

When Mrs Matthews's old father died, she inherited his gold watch, which had belonged to his father and grandfather before him. It was big and heavy and worth a lot of money, but it was broken, so Mrs Matthews took it to be repaired.

The man in the jeweller's shop was very interested to see such an unusual watch, and when he had examined its insides, he said he could certainly have it repaired for her. 'It'll last a long time once that's been done,' he said. He wrote out a ticket and gave it to Mrs Matthews saying, 'Please bring this when you come to pick up the watch. But it might take a bit of time, because it isn't a modern watch.'

But Mrs Matthews had a lot of things to think about after her father died. She had to arrange to sell his little house, and to deal with his money affairs, write to her brother in Australia and so on.

The result was that she completely forgot about the watch that she had taken in for repair, and about the ticket for it, which she had put away in a drawer to keep it safe.

Then, while she was looking through some old drawers one day, she found the ticket for the watch repair.

'What's this?' she said to herself. 'A ticket for a watch repair? Who took a watch in to be repaired? And why didn't they give this ticket in when they went to pick it up?'

She thought back, and suddenly she remembered. 'My father's gold watch!' she thought. 'Didn't I pick it up? When did I take it in?' She looked at the ticket again.

'How old's this ticket?' she said to herself. It was five years old. Mrs Matthews had heard that shops could sell things that people had left with them if they didn't pick them up and pay for them before a certain time. 'But the watch might still be there,' she thought. 'I'll go and see if I can get it back. It might have been sold, but I hope not.'

She took the ticket to the jeweller's the next time she went out shopping, and the shopkeeper looked at it and then went to look for the watch without saying a word.

'That's good,' Mrs Matthews thought. 'He didn't seem to mind about the date.'

The man came back after a few minutes and said, 'It won't be ready until Friday.'

Exercise 1

Look at these questions. Find the right answers. Then write the questions and the answers:

1 Why did the jeweller's shop in Mrs Matthews's town not employ an expert watch repairer?
   a) Because he worked in London.   b) Because there was not enough work for one.
2 Why did Mrs Matthews take the gold watch to the shop?
   a) Because it was big and heavy.   b) Because it was broken.
3 Did the man in the shop think the watch was worth repairing?
   a) No, he did not.   b) Yes, but he was doubtful.
   c) Yes, he thought it was very worth repairing.
4 Why did he give Mrs Matthews a ticket?
   a) Because it might take a bit of time.   b) So that he could give the watch to the right person when it was ready.
5 Why was Mrs Matthews surprised when she found the ticket in a drawer?
   a) Because nobody had taken the ticket when they went to pick up the watch.   b) Because she had forgotten about the watch.

Further stories
for reading comprehension A

Answer key

Please unbend staples carefully and detach this key.

ANSWER KEY

Exercise 1: 1b, 2a, 3a, 4a, 5a, 6b, 7b, 8b, 9b, 10a
Exercise 2: 1 'The school is a few kilometres away.' 2 'Pupils can get there on the school bus.' 3 'They come home on the school bus too.' 4 'The place where Mary can get the bus is twenty metres from her home.' 5 'She has to be there by half past eight.' 6 'The bus is usually on time, and it is never more than a minute or two late.' 7 'Mary was not on the bus this morning because her mother's alarm clock failed to go off.' 8 'Her mother drove her to school in her car.' 9 'Her mother did not know the way.' 10 'She managed to get there because Mary showed her the way.' 11 'When she got there, she asked Mary why she had made her go such a long way round instead of the most direct way.' 12 'Mary answered that it was because she didn't know how else to get there.'
Exercise 3: 1 Why ever did they do that? 2 How ever did that happen? 3 Where ever did she find that? 4 What ever did she do that for? 5 When ever did she find time for that? 6 Who ever told her that?

Exercise 1: 1b, 2a, 3b, 4a, 5b, 6b, 7a, 8a, 9b, 10a
Exercise 2: 1 studying 2 artist 3 usual 4 shopping 5 colourful 6 useless 7 smallness 8 tearfully 9 addressed 10 birthday
Exercise 3: 1 had been studying 2 had finished 3 had been living 4 had bought 5 had gone 6 had been sitting 7 had been reading 8 had lost

Exercise 1: 1b, 2a, 3a, 4a, 5a, 6b, 7b, 8a, 9b, 10b
Exercise 2: she was a careful driver, she was rather late, another car coming in the opposite direction, to waste on an accident, a very important appointment in town at nine, was busy too, go away in their cars and then come back to the scene of the accident in the evening and put them in exactly the same positions as they were in then, to the place where the accident had happened, was waiting there in his car, in exactly the same positions as they had been in after the accident, the telephone in her car, the police
Exercise 3: 1 will be working 2 will finish, will see 3 will drive, will be waiting 4 will still be living 5 will be staying 6 will not finish, will still be eating

Exercise 1: 1a, 2b, 3a, 4b, 5b, 6b, 7a, 8b, 9a, 10a
Exercise 2: 1 seriousness 2 death 3 accidentally 4 forceful 5 dangerously 6 personal 7 freedom 8 refusal 9 sensible 10 crash
Exercise 3: 1 may have 2 may have fallen 3 may have been 4 may

swim 5 may owe 6 may have been 7 may have knocked, may be 8 may save

UNIT 5

Exercise 1: 1c, 2b, 3b, 4a, 5a, 6b, 7b, 8a, 9b, 10a
Exercise 2: Jack was a schoolboy. He always had a lot of homework, but he put off doing it every day because he wanted to watch television. At first his mother let him do this. The result was that Jack was too tired to do his homework properly, if at all. Then his mother began to make him do it first. The result was that Jack did the work quickly and carelessly in order to finish it and get back to his beloved television. Then his mother began to test him when he finished. One day this was less difficult than usual because Jack's homework had a strong connection with television. The next day the teacher asked Jack what some of the things were that Thomas Edison had done for science, and Jack answered that, if it hadn't been for Edison, they would all be watching television by candlelight.
Exercise 3: 1 Most children begin watching television when they are very young, and continue watching it all their lives. 2 Other children enjoy playing games instead. 3 Some adults try making children do their homework instead, and sometimes they are successful. 4 Some children do not seem to mind doing a lot of homework. 5 Other children prefer watching television. 6 I remember not having television when I was a child. 7 I shall never forget writing my own stories and drawing pictures for them. 8 I shall never stop doing this.

UNIT 6

Exercise 1: 1b, 2b, 3b, 4b, 5b, 6a, 7b, 8b, 9b, 10a
Exercise 2: 1 writer 2 novelist 3 disappointment 4 invitation 5 eagerness 6 photographer 7 excitement 8 lucky 9 interesting 10 advice
Exercise 3: 1 Violet told Alan that Fraser Lambourn was coming to the bookshop soon, and that he was going to sign copies of his new book. 2 Alan told Violet that she had already brought him a copy of his new book. 3 Violet said that Fraser had been telling her about his early days as a writer, and that it had been most interesting. 4 Fraser said that his real name was Larry Lamb, but his agent had advised him to change it. 5 Alan told a friend that his wife worked in a bookshop.

UNIT 7

Exercise 1: 1b, 2a, 3b, 4a, 5b, 6b, 7a, 8a, 9a, 10a
Exercise 2: Joan likes her work very much. Her computers answer her just like people, but more politely and without arguing, and without one having to wonder whether one is going to hurt their feelings, and without ever lying. Joan's mother thought that they sounded like perfect companions or husbands. She wanted advice from a computer about which of her two watches to keep, the one that gained a second

every hour, or the one that had stopped. The computer advised her to keep the one that had stopped, because it would be right once every twelve hours, but the other one would be right only once every five years.

Exercise 3: 1 so 2 so 3 not 4 so 5 not 6 so

UNIT **8**

Exercise 1: 1b, 2b, 3b, 4b, 5c, 6a, 7a, 8a, 9a, 10a
Exercise 2: 1 shortness 2 scientific, scientists 3 frozen 4 dusty 5 beginning(s) 6 valuable 7 discoveries 8 truth 9 agreement 10 prove
Exercise 3: 1 It, there 2 It, there 3 There, it 4 There, it

UNIT **9**

Exercise 1: 1a, 2b, 3a, 4a, 5a, 6a, 7b, 8b, 9b, 10b
Exercise 2: her husband, they had had to look after their animals every day, two of their children, who had stayed on on the farm after leaving school, ran it for them for two weeks, to go to Bournemouth, to do some sightseeing, for their sightseeing trips, maps, the way to the hotel, a nice policeman, just behind the hotel, go sightseeing that day, about to leave the room, a notice on the inside of the door of their room, of meals, disappointed, that they did not allow them much time for sightseeing, he thought that they had to sit in the dining room during the whole meal times shown
Exercise 3: 1 Mr and Mrs Jones had to look after the animals (that were) on their farm. 2 The people who looked after the farm when Mr and Mrs Jones were away were their children. 3 The hotel (that) Mr and Mrs Jones had chosen was near the sea. 4 The people (whom) Mr and Mrs Jones saw were bathing, playing games or just lying on the beach.

UNIT **10**

Exercise 1: 1b, 2b, 3c, 4b, 5b, 6b, 7a, 8b, 9c, 10a
Exercise 2: 1 life 2 gold 3 heaviness 4 jewellery 5 worthless 6 repair 7 repairer 8 arrangements 9 payment 10 hope
Exercise 3: 1 This shop might repair your watch quickly, but I am doubtful. 2 Mrs Matthews's great-grandfather might have owned the gold watch too. 3 Mrs Matthews might have forgotten about the watch for ever. 4 '. . . I might get the watch back, but it might have been sold.'

UNIT **11**

Exercise 1: 1b, 2b, 3b, 4a, 5b, 6a, 7b, 8b, 9a, 10b
Exercise 2: Sally had always loved trees and flowers. It had been difficult for her to have an English garden before because of the heat and dryness of the countries she had worked in. She was at last able

to have one when she came back to England to live. She wanted a house near a shop for when she was too old to drive her car any more. The garden of the house she bought needed a lot of work because it had not been very well looked after by the last owners. She did not use chemicals to kill weeds because they also killed some of the birds and butterflies she loved to see. She kept some weeds because some kinds of butterflies liked them very much. A magazine suggested that if you think nice thoughts about your plants and really love them, they will grow better, but if you think bad thoughts about them, they will never get big and strong. Sally's sister Alice said that people who believed this idea unfortunately never explained why most of the weeds grew so well when people hated them so much.
Exercise 3: 1 Most 2 any, some 3 any 4 none 5 none of 6 Most of 7 any of, some of

UNIT **12**

Exercise 1: 1b, 2b, 3c, 4a, 5a, 6b, 7b, 8a, 9b, 10b
Exercise 2: 1 inventor 2 information 3 wasteful 4 difficulty 5 correctness 6 gatherings 7 cleverness 8 producers
Exercise 3: 1 as, as, less, than, so, that 2 more, than, so, that, less, than

UNIT **13**

Exercise 1: 1a, 2a, 3a, 4b, 5a, 6a, 7b, 8c, 9b, 10b
Exercise 2: The Greenville park now closes at six every evening. The council met to discuss whether, in the summer, the playground should be left open till later. Some members thought that children should not be encouraged to stay out late in the evenings. Other members said that it was healthy for children to have a change from television, to get some fresh air, and to be able to play in the playground instead of perhaps doing things that were either dangerous or harmful. One member mentioned the danger of a child being taken away by some horrible man, but according to another member, this danger could be avoided by parents going with their children. One member had seen groups of children playing in the playground after six every evening. They got in by climbing through small holes in the fence. That was a good thing because it was much more exciting for them to do things they thought were forbidden. The council agreed to continue to close the gates at six so as not to spoil the children's fun.
Exercise 3: 1 The park had always been closed at six. 2 Now people thought it should be closed later, and this was discussed a lot. 3 A man said, 'Damage is done and windows are broken at night.' 4 A woman said, 'Children have been seen in the playground after six.' 5 The members of the town council said, 'The gates will continue to be closed at six.'

ANSWER KEY

UNIT **14**

Exercise 1: 1b, 2b, 3a, 4a, 5b, 6a, 7a, 8a, 9b, 10a
Exercise 2: 1 nastiness 2 violence 3 gardener 4 protection 5 cyclist
6 cloudy 7 entertainment 8 listener 9 rudeness 10 refusal
Exercise 3: 1 interested,   interesting   2 astonishing,   Astonished
3 breaking, broken 4 tired, tiring 5 surprising, surprised

UNIT **15**

Exercise 1: 1b, 2a, 3a, 4a, 5a, 6a, 7a, 8b, 9a, 10a
Exercise 2: go to various parts of the country, visiting factories, offices
and shops and trying to get them to buy the things the company
makes, in hotels, by train and taxi, is needed by her mother and father
to take the children to school, a five per cent commission, she is paid
her travel and living expenses, being away from her family at night,
the extra money for meals away is not much comfort, would probably
be willing to *pay* the company if that allowed them the pleasure of
getting away from home, a claim for an amount of £203.22, it was a
mistake, it was her hotel bill, it would be nice if she did not buy any
more hotels the next time she went to Manchester
Exercise 3: 1 would be, snowed 2 would have gone, had had 3 would
go, bought 4 would enjoy, went 5 would have had, had not eaten
6 would have spent, had gone

UNIT **16**

Exercise 1: 1a, 2b, 3a, 4a, 5b, 6a, 7a, 8a, 9b, 10a
Exercise 2: 1 traveller   2 Wooden   3 hopeless   4 scenery   5 tiring
6 foolishly 7 sickness 8 smoothness 9 effortless 10 mysterious
Exercise 3: 1 I used to stand on a truck, pretending it was moving.
2 I used to travel from London, taking my younger brothers with me.
3 Other passengers came into the compartment, carrying a lot of
luggage. 4 I sat outside the station restaurant, eating a big dinner.
5 One can go along to the dining car and have a meal, taking as much
time as one wants.

UNIT **17**

Exercise 1: 1a, 2b, 3a, 4a, 5a, 6a, 7a, 8b, 9a, 10a
Exercise 2: Dave retired when he was sixty-five. He decided to visit
a safari park because he had always been interested in wild animals.
His friend Joe wanted to go with him, and Dave agreed as he was
often lonely, and did not much enjoy doing things by himself. The
tickets cost five pounds each, but Dave and Joe could get in at half
price by showing their pension cards. Joe had a part-time job in an
amusement arcade. He got a lot of coins one Friday evening because
one of his jobs was to take the money out of the various games
machines there. He could not take them to the bank until Monday
because it was closed on Saturdays and Sundays, so he decided to pay

for his and Dave's tickets with some of them. When the ticket seller saw the coins, he thought they had been saving up for a long time to come to the safari park!

Exercise 3: 1 So does Joe. 2 So are leopards. 3 Neither/Nor can Dave. 4 So had Joe. 5 Neither/Nor do children. 6 Neither/Nor will Joe.

UNIT **18**

Exercise 1: 1b, 2a, 3b, 4a, 5a, 6b, 7a, 8b, 9a, 10b
Exercise 2: 1 fast 2 policeman/policewoman 3 enjoyment 4 carefully 5 driver 6 speeding 7 warnings 8 darkness
Exercise 3: 1 unless 2 if 3 when 4 When 5 If

UNIT **19**

Exercise 1: 1a, 2a, 3a, 4a, 5a, 6b, 7a, 8b, 9b, 10b
Exercise 2: Peter's mother taught him to drive a car. He did not have lessons from a driving instructor because his wages were not high enough to pay one. His mother bought him his first car. He had to pay for the licence, insurance, petrol and so on. His mother suggested that he should learn everything about his engine so that he could do something about it if necessary, but he did not do it because he found it too difficult to understand the detailed instructions in the book he had. While he was driving in the country one day a red light suddenly came on in the car and it slowly came to a stop. Peter opened the bonnet and checked the petrol supply. Then suddenly he heard a cough near his left ear. An old horse had made the noise. It said, 'You'd better have a look at the sparking plugs.' Peter ran to a farm a few hundred metres down the road and told a farmer what had happened. He answered, 'You'd better not listen to him. He doesn't know much about cars.'
Exercise 3: 1 Peter has a small secondhand car, but he would rather have a big new one. 2 He had better learn about the engine of his car before it is too late. 3 He had better drive carefully if he wants to avoid accidents. 4 He would rather drive fast, but he knows he had better not. 5 The farmer told him that he had better not listen to the old horse's advice.

UNIT **20**

Exercise 1: 1a, 2b, 3b, 4a, 5a, 6a, 7b, 8b, 9b, 10b
Exercise 2: 1 beauties 2 tightness 3 comfort 4 breath 5 swimmer 6 nervousness 7 protection 8 effortlessly 9 fierceness 10 divers
Exercise 3: 1 We use aqualungs in order to stay under water for a long time, but we use snorkels in order to save money. 2 A snorkel has a curved tube in order to be held in one's teeth at one end and at the same time stick up out of the water at the other. 3 You have to blow out of the tube in order to start breathing through it. 4 I went to Fiji in order to work there.

6   What could shops do if things were not picked up and
    paid for?
    a) Leave things with them.   b) Sell them.
7   Did the shopkeeper make trouble when Mrs Matthews
    took the ticket in?
    a) No, he did not.   b) Yes, he did.
8   Why did he not bring the watch to Mrs Matthews when
    he came back?
    a) Because it had been sold.   b) Because it was not yet
    ready.
9   How old was the ticket?
    a) Five days.   b) Five months.   c) Five years.
10 Was it reasonable for a watch to take so long to repair?
    a) No, it was not.   b) Yes, it was.

Exercise 2

In each of these (pairs of) sentences fill the empty space with
a word that has the same root as the word *in italics*:

1   Mrs Matthews *lived* in a small town. She had been there
    all her . . . .
2   We can say, 'Mrs Matthews inherited a watch that was
    made of *gold*' or 'Mrs Matthews inherited a . . . watch.'
3   The watch was unusually *heavy*. Some people would not
    have liked to wear it because of its . . . .
4   One doesn't only find watches in a *jeweller's* shop; . . . is
    another of the things it will sell.
5   The watch was *worth* a lot of money. Even if it had not
    been possible to repair it, it would still not have been
    . . . because it was made of gold.
6   We can say, 'Mrs Matthews took the watch in to be
    repaired' or 'Mrs Matthews took the watch in for . . .'.
7   A person who *repairs* watches is called a watch . . . .
8   We can say, 'Mrs Matthews *arranged* to sell her father's
    house' or 'Mrs Matthews made all the . . . for selling her
    father's house.'
9   We can say, 'A shop can demand that it should be *paid*
    within a certain time' or 'A shop can demand that . . .
    should be made within a certain time.'
10 Mrs Matthews *hoped* the shop had not sold the watch. She
    took the ticket along in the . . . of getting it back.

Exercise 3

'She *might do* it' is used instead of 'She *may do* it' (see Unit 4) to mean 'It is possible that she does (or will do) it', but *might do* it shows a lesser possibility than *may do*. 'She *might have done* it' means 'It is possible that she did it at a time in the past.' Again, the possibility is less than with *may have done*.

Change these sentences by using a verb with *might* instead of 'it is possible that' or 'perhaps':

1 It is possible that this shop will repair your watch quickly, but I am doubtful.
2 Perhaps Mrs Matthews's great-grandfather owned the gold watch too.
3 It is possible that Mrs Matthews could have forgotten about the watch for ever.
4 When she found the ticket, Mrs Matthews said to herself, 'Perhaps I will get the watch back, but it is possible that it has been sold.'

Sally had lived abroad most of her life, but at last she came back to England to live. She had always loved trees and flowers, and now she aimed to buy a small house in the country with a garden. She had managed to save quite a lot of money while working in hospitals in foreign countries, so she hoped to be able to buy something nice.

'You know,' she said to her sister Alice, 'it was very difficult indeed to have an English garden in any of the countries I worked in, because of the heat and the dryness.'

Alice, who was not at all interested in gardens and preferred life indoors, pretended to be sympathetic, but she was secretly thinking that it would be nice to live in a country where one had none of the troubles she had with her garden.

But Sally continued to be keen, and soon she had found a suitable place in a nice row of houses at the edge of a small village with quite a big garden. 'I very much wanted a place near a village shop,' she said to Alice, 'chiefly for when I'm too old to drive my car any more.'

Sally moved into her new house, and began to work on the garden. It had not been very well looked after by the last owners, so that the grass on the lawn was rough and in need of a lot of work, and the whole garden was full of weeds. It was a big job to make everything look as neat as Sally wanted it to be, especially as she could not afford to employ a gardener, and she was very much against chemicals to kill weeds, as they also killed some of the birds and butterflies she loved to see.

At last she had got rid of most of the weeds, except in one corner of her garden, where she allowed them to grow freely behind a hedge because some kinds of butterflies liked them very much.

'Do you know,' she said to Alice, 'there are so few suitable weeds for certain butterflies in any of the gardens in this part of the country that they have almost disappeared here.'

'And I read in a magazine,' answered Alice, 'that some people believe that, if you think nice thoughts about your plants and really love them, they will grow much better, but if you think bad thoughts about them, they will never get big and strong. Unfortunately, people who believe this never explain why most of the weeds grow so well when people hate them so much.'

Exercise 1

Look at these questions. Find the right answers. Then write the questions and the answers:

1 Why did Sally want a garden?
   a) Because she had come back to live in England.
   b) Because she loved trees and flowers.
2 How had she managed to save money to buy a house and garden?
   a) By living in England.   b) By working abroad.
3 Why could she not have an English garden easily abroad?
   a) Because she worked in hospitals.   b) Because she worked in hot dry places.
4 Did Alice like gardens as much as her sister?
   a) No, she did not.   b) No, she liked them more.
   c) Yes, she did.
5 Why did Sally want a house near a village?
   a) Because she could have quite a big garden there.
   b) So as to be able to shop easily when she was too old to drive.
6 Was the garden in good condition when Sally bought it?
   a) No, it was not.   b) Yes, it was.
7 Did she have a gardener?
   a) No, she did not, because she enjoyed doing the work herself.   b) No, she did not, because she was not rich enough.   c) Yes, she did.
8 Why did she leave some weeds?
   a) Because she did not want to use chemicals.   b) For the birds and butterflies.
9 What do some people think about plants?
   a) That if one loves them, they grow better.   b) That if one hates weeds, it will help them to grow well.
10 What mistake do these people make?
   a) They do not love their plants enough.   b) They do not see that the weeds they hate grow very well.

Exercise 2

Guided summary. Write a summary of the above story by answering these questions. Do not use numbers:

1   What had Sally always loved? (*Sally had* . . .)
2   Why had it been difficult for her to have an English garden before?
3   When was she at last able to have one?
4   Why did she want a house near a shop?
5   Why did the garden of the house she bought need a lot of work?
6   Why did she not use chemicals to kill weeds?
7   Why did she keep some weeds?
8   How did a magazine suggest one could grow plants better?
9   What did Sally's sister Alice say about this?

Exercise 3

> *Some, any* and *most* can be used as pronouns (e.g. Sally hasn't got vegetables in her garden, and she wants some. She also wants flowers, but she hasn't got any yet. She has a lot of trees, but most are very small). Instead of the adjective *no* (e.g. She has no weeds) the pronoun *none* is used (e.g. There are weeds behind the hedge, but none in front of it).
>
> The pronouns *some, any, most* and *none* can be followed by *of* + a noun or pronoun (phrase) (e.g. She has a lot of grass, but some of it is dead. Has Sally got any of these kinds of trees? Most of the houses here are too expensive for Sally. None of these butterflies like weeds).

Put *any, most, none* or *some* in each space in these sentences. Put *of* in too, if this is necessary:

1   Sally worked in a lot of foreign countries. . . . were too hot for an English garden, but one or two were too dry.
2   Alice asked Sally, 'Have you got weeds in your lawn still?' 'No,' answered Sally, 'I haven't got . . . there, but I've got . . . behind a hedge, for the birds and butterflies.'
3   Sally said to Alice, 'I need some seeds. Have you got . . . in your garden?'
4   'Are there any shops in Sally's street?' 'No, there are . . . .'
5   Sally likes birds, but there were . . . the rare ones in her village till she let some weeds grow for them.
6   . . . the people in Sally's village are farmers, but one or two are not.
7   Sally did not choose . . . the many houses she found in towns, although . . . them (three in fact) were nice.

41

When the steam engine was invented in the eighteenth century, it began one of the greatest revolutions that have ever happened in our world. The invention of the petrol engine at the end of the nineteenth century led to another enormous change in our lives. And the computer is almost certainly going to be no less important an invention than these engines were.

Just as there was a Stone Age, an Iron Age and so on, we have been living for centuries in a Paper Age, during which almost all information was kept and sent on paper; and so much of it is wasted after it has been used once that enormous numbers of trees have to be cut down every year to provide us with this paper. But now, with the computer, enormous amounts of information can be stored and sent without any paper at all, using small discs or magnetic tape.

When computers began, they were very big machines, because information had to be stored on large spools of tape. But since then, ways have been found of storing more and more information in smaller and smaller areas by electronic means, until now an up-to-date computer can be so small that one can carry it in one's briefcase.

Computers have also made it possible to do very difficult calculations very much faster than any earlier machine could. One has to programme one's computer correctly, of course, feeding into it the facts one wants it to work on, and telling it what one wants it to do with them, but after that, the process can be very fast.

Computers also allow one to send information to others anywhere in the world, using ordinary telephones, and to receive information from them. One can send a very long message more quickly from England to Australia, for example, than from one's house to someone in one's garden, and the computer at the other end will remember it, ready for printing out when one wants.

Computers are not only used for writing; they can produce diagrams and pictures, and they can be used for playing games. One now sees them at airports and railway stations, in hotels and restaurants; in fact, almost everywhere that people gather. A lot of people, mostly young ones, also have their own computers on which they can play games.

Computers need programmes, sometimes also called software. These tell the computer what to do, and the great progress that is being made in the field of computers is not only in the hardware – the machines themselves – but also in the art of programming. Clever people are finding more and more things for computers to do, but the people who produce the programmes that make these things possible still have to be as clever as – or cleverer than – the programmes they produce.

Exercise 1

Look at these questions. Find the right answers. Then write the questions and the answers:

1   What eighteenth-century invention greatly changed the world?
    a) The great revolution.   b) The steam engine.
2   What brought about another great revolution at the end of the nineteenth century?
    a) An enormous change in our lives.   b) The petrol engine.
3   How does the computer compare with the steam engine and the petrol engine?
    a) It is probably less important. b) It is certainly more important. c) It will probably be as important.
4   Why is the Paper Age doing a lot of harm?
    a) Because it leads to a lot of wood from trees being wasted.   b) Because it leads to too much information being kept.
5   What does the computer store information on?
    a) Discs and tape. b) Paper.

6 Are computers getting bigger or smaller?
 a) Bigger. b) Smaller.
7 How can one send messages quickly from England to Australia?
 a) By sending them from one's garden. b) By using a computer and a telephone.
8 Where can one find machines for computer games?
 a) In a lot of places where people meet. b) In places where young people play football.
9 What is software?
 a) The computer machines. b) The programmes used in computers.
10 Who makes the software?
 a) Artists. b) Clever people.

Exercise 2

In each of these (pairs of) sentences fill the empty space with a word that has the same root as the one *in italics*:

1 A person who *invents* something is called an . . ..
2 'Did you *inform* all the students about the arrival of the new computer?' 'Yes, I sent out the . . . yesterday.'
3 'We *waste* an enormous amount of paper.' 'Yes, and we are also terribly . . . with glass.'
4 We can say, 'Do you find such calculations *difficult*?' or we can say, 'Do you have . . . with such calculations?'
5 We can say, 'You have to check whether your programme is *correct*' or 'You have to check the . . . of your programme.'
6 We can say, 'We can find computer games wherever people *gather*' or 'We can find computer games wherever there are . . . of people.'
7 We can say, 'A programme depends on how *clever* the programmer is' or 'A programme depends on the . . . of the programmer.'
8 We can say, 'We need people who can *produce* new programmes' or 'We need . . . of new programmes.'

Exercise 3

> To show that two or more things are equally large, or go equally quickly etc., we can use *as . . . as . . .* (e.g. My computer is as small as yours, and it works as quickly as my brother's).
>
> To show that someone/something is bigger, or goes faster etc. than someone/something else, we can use *more . . . than . . .* (e.g. My computer is more powerful than yours, and it works more quickly than my friend's).
>
> To show that someone/something is not as big, or does not go as fast etc. as someone/something else, we can use *less . . . than . . .* (e.g. Discs are less wasteful than paper).
>
> To show the result of something, we can use *so . . . that . . .* (e.g. This computer is so small that it can go in a briefcase).

Put *as, less, more, so, than* or *that* in each empty space in these sentences:

1 The petrol engine was . . . important an invention . . . the steam engine, and the computer is also very important indeed. In fact, it is no . . . important . . . either of them. It is . . . important . . . it will change our lives completely.
2 The petrol engine made it possible for us to travel . . . quickly . . . the steam engine could carry us. It worked . . . well . . . it made air journeys possible. The steam engine worked . . . well . . . the petrol engine, so we have never had steam planes!

Greenville was a small town in the middle of England. Most of it was full of houses and shops, but in the middle of the town there was a small park, which contained, among other things, a playground for small children. The park had always been closed at six every evening, and this had meant that the playground closed at that time too, but now the town council was discussing whether, in the summer, the playground should be left open till later.

There was a lot of discussion about this among the members of the town council. A few of them thought that children should not be encouraged to stay out late in the evenings; others said that it was healthy for children to have a change from television, to get some fresh air, and to be able to play in the playground instead of perhaps doing things that were either dangerous or harmful.

'I'm ashamed to say,' said one man, 'that bored children often don't behave themselves. Some of them go about doing damage, or they fight and get into trouble. They break windows and paint rude signs on walls, and perhaps start taking drugs. It's much better for them to be given swings and slides and other things that interest them in a healthy way, isn't it?'

'But what about the danger of a child being taken away by some horrible man?' asked another member of the town council anxiously. 'One hears about it now and again in other towns, you know!'

'Yes, I agree with you,' the first man said. 'That's a good argument. Well, parents would have to go with their children in that case.'

Then another of the members spoke. 'Have any of you ever gone to the playground on a summer evening?' she asked. 'If you had, you would have seen that there are groups of children playing there after six every evening.'

'But the playground isn't open then!' a man said.

'I know,' the woman answered, 'but it's no mystery that there are plenty of small holes in the fence round the playground through which the children can climb. And when they have to get in that way, they're much more eager to do so than if the gates are open. It's much more exciting for them to do things they think are forbidden, you see, and it does no harm, does it?'

The other members of the town council laughed, and they all agreed that the gates should continue to be closed at six for the children's sake, so as not to spoil their fun.

Exercise 1

Look at these questions. Find the right answers. Then write the questions and the answers:

1 What was in the small park in Greenville?
   a) A playground for small children.   b) Lots of houses and shops.

2 What time were the town council thinking of closing the park?
   a) After six.   b) At six.   c) Before six.

3 Why did some of the members not want to change the time?
   a) Because they did not want children to stay out late.
   b) Because they wanted children not to watch so much television.

4 Why did others want the park to remain open later?
   a) To encourage children to stop going out. b) To stop children doing dangerous and harmful things.

5 What danger did one member of the town council see if the park was left open later?
   a) The danger that a child might be taken away by a stranger. b) The danger of taking drugs.

6 How did another member suggest this could be avoided?
   a) By getting parents to go with their children. b) By closing the park earlier.

7 At what time had one member seen children playing in the playground?
   a) Earlier than six. b) Later than six.

8 How had they got in?
   a) By going in before six. b) Over the fence. c) Through the fence.

9 Why was that a good thing?
   a) Because it kept the children from harm. b) Because it was exciting for them.

10 Why did the town council agree to continue closing the park at six?
   a) Because of the dangers of leaving it open later. b) So that the children could still enjoy getting in through the fence.

Exercise 2

Guided summary. You are a newspaper reporter who has to write an article about the meeting of the Greenville town council which is the subject of the above story.

Say:
when the Greenville park closes now.
what the council met to discuss.
what some members thought about children staying out late.
what other members thought about this.
what danger one member mentioned.
how this danger could be avoided, according to another member.
what another member had seen on summer evenings.
how the children got in.
why that was a good thing.
what the council agreed to do, and why.

Exercise 3

When we are more interested in the person, animal or thing who/that something happens **to**, and in **what** happens to her/him/it, than we are in the person, animal or thing who/that **does** the action, we often use the passive instead of the active (e.g. instead of saying, 'Something stung me on the face last night' I say 'I was stung on the face last night', because I am not interested in **what** stung me, but in what happened **to me**). If we want, we can say who or what did the action by using *by* + noun/pronoun (phrase) (e.g. 'I was stung by a bee').

Write these sentences again, making the word(s) *in italics* the subject. Do not use *by*:

1 They had always closed *the park* at six.
2 Now people thought they should close *it* later, and they discussed *this* a lot.
3 A man said, 'People do *damage* and break *windows* at night.'
4 A woman said, 'People have seen *children* in the playground after six.'
5 The members of the town council said, 'We will continue to close *the gates* at six.'

Norah had a cottage on a cliff above a big bay. In winter it could be very nasty because of strong winds and sea spray. In fact, when a gale was blowing, Norah and her husband got used to sleeping in a small room downstairs, because their bedroom upstairs, which faced the gales, had a very big window, and they were afraid that an extra violent gust might break it and blow pieces of broken glass over them.

Also, the salt spray from the sea put an end to many of the colourful plants Norah planted in her garden. She tried putting up a fence to protect them, but the wind just hit it, went up over the top and then down the other side, so in the end she filled the garden with trees and bushes that liked salt.

But most of the summer Norah enjoyed her cottage and garden very much. At weekends she could sit out-of-doors in the sun, looking at the beautiful view, with interesting ships and boats passing by, and she could very easily cycle down to the sea for a swim.

Now, Norah and her husband had plenty of friends and relations. These people never came to visit them in winter, when it was wet and cloudy, and the weather did not make the position of the cottage on the coast very nice, but in the summer lots of them used to come to enjoy the beautiful place, and in the end it really became quite annoying for Norah and her husband. When they were at home, they found friends and relations arriving, expecting to be given unlimited drinks and meals, and to sit in the sun for hours, talking as if Norah and her husband had nothing else to do but entertain and listen to them.

This went on for several years. Norah did not wish to appear rude by refusing to let her friends and relations in, but on the other hand, she was getting tired every summer.

Then one day Norah was complaining about this to her hairdresser while she was doing her hair.

'You're disturbed by too many uninvited guests, are you?' said the hairdresser. 'Why don't you try my way of escaping?'

'What's that?' asked Norah.

'Well,' the hairdresser answered, 'when the bell rings, I put on my coat and take my shopping bag. If it's someone I don't want to see, I say innocently, "I'm sorry, but I've got to go out." But if it's someone I want to see, I say, "How lucky! I've just come in!"'

Exercise 1

Look at these questions. Find the right answers. Then write the questions and the answers:

1 What were the bad things about Norah's cottage?
   a) The fact that it was on a cliff and above a big bay.
   b) The gales and salt spray.
2 Where did Norah and her husband usually sleep?
   a) In a small room downstairs.   b) Upstairs.
3 When did they not sleep there?
   a) When there was a gale.   b) When there was an extra violent gust.
4 Why did Norah fill her garden with trees and bushes that liked salt?
   a) Because other ones were killed by salt spray.
   b) Because their fruits tasted better.

5 Why did friends and relations only come in the summer?
   a) Because Norah and her husband were at home then.
   b) Because they did not like the weather in the winter.
6 What made Norah tired?
   a) Feeding and talking to lots of guests.   b) Refusing to
   let her friends and relations in.
7 Who gave her some advice about this?
   a) A hairdresser.   b) Some uninvited guests.
8 What did her hairdresser do when a guest arrived?
   a) She got ready to go out.   b) She rang the bell.
9 What did she do if she did not want the guest to come in?
   a) She said that the guest had to go out.   b) She said she
   had to go out.
10 And what did she say if she wanted the guest to come in?
   a) She said that she had just returned home.   b) She said
   that the guest was a lucky person.

Exercise 2

In each of these (pairs of) sentences fill the empty space with
a word that has the same root as the word *in italics*:

1 The weather was often *nasty* in winter, but Norah forgot
   its . . . in the summer.
2 The gales on the cliff could be very *violent*. Their . . . sometimes forced Norah and her husband to sleep downstairs.
3 Norah did all the work in her *garden* because her husband
   was useless as a . . . .
4 She tried to *protect* her plants with a fence, but it proved
   to be no . . . at all.
5 She *cycled* a lot in the summer, because she had always
   been a keen . . . .
6 There were often black *clouds* in the sky in winter, but they
   did not often have . . . days in the summer.
7 Norah did not mind *entertaining* relations and friends once
   a week, but they expected . . . almost every day in the
   summer.
8 Norah did not enjoy *listening* to long stories, because she
   was not really a good . . . .
9 She did not like being *rude* to her visitors, because she
   disliked . . . in other people so much.
10 She did not like to *refuse* to let her friends and relations
   in, because she knew they would be hurt by such a . . . .

Exercise 3

> The -*ing* form can be used to form adjectives from verbs; it then describes the person or thing 'who/that does the action of the verb' (e.g. 'This story excites people' can become 'This is an exciting story').
>
> The past participle can also be used as an adjective; it then describes the person or thing 'to whom/which the action of the verb is done' (e.g. we can say, 'The play in this theatre is exciting the children' and 'There are a lot of excited children in this theatre').

Write these sentences, changing the verbs in brackets into the -*ing* form or past participle:

1 Norah was (interest) in trees, and she had some (interest) ones in her garden.
2 The violence of the gales was quite (astonish). (astonish) people used to see them breaking windows and doors.
3 One very windy night Norah heard the sound of (break) glass upstairs, and when she went to look, she found a (break) window.
4 Norah was (tire) every day in the summer because it was (tire) having so many guests.
5 Norah's hairdresser made a (surprise) suggestion. Norah was quite (surprise) to hear it.

Freda Livingstone was a saleswoman. She had just begun to work for a big company that employed a lot of salesmen and saleswomen. They had to go to various parts of the country, visiting factories, offices and shops and trying to get them to buy the things the company made. Of course while they were away they had to live in hotels. Some of them used their own cars, and others travelled by train and taxi.

Freda lived with her parents. She had married young and had two children, but then her husband had died, so she had returned to her old home so that her mother and father could help with the children while she went out to work. She thought this would be especially useful when she was away travelling for her company. Then she would leave her car at home so that her mother or father could take the children to school in it, while she herself went by train, although she would have preferred to go by car if she had not had any children.

'It would be more comfortable if I could do that,' she thought. 'Well, later, perhaps, when the children are a bit older, they can go to school by bus, and I can take the car when I have to travel.'

Freda and the other salespeople in her company were not only paid a salary; they also got a five per cent commission on every sale they were able to make, and they were paid their travel and living expenses while they were away from home on company business. Those who went by train got back the cost of their tickets and taxis, and those who travelled in their own cars could claim a petrol allowance for each mile.

Freda hated being away from her family at night, so the extra money for meals away was not much comfort, but she realised that some other people would probably have been willing to *pay* the company if that had allowed them the pleasure of getting away from home!

One day some time after her first business trip, Freda was

sent for by the manager of the company, Helena Wright. Helena said to her, 'I've been looking at your expense claims, Freda. When you went to Manchester earlier this month, you claimed one amount of £203.22. Is that a mistake?'

'Oh, no!' Freda answered. 'That was my hotel bill.'

'Then it would be nice,' Helena said, 'if you did not buy any more hotels the next time you went to Manchester.'

Exercise 1

Look at these questions. Find the right answers. Then write the questions and the answers:

1 What was Freda Livingstone's work?
   a) She employed a lot of salesmen and saleswomen.
   b) She travelled around selling things.
2 Why did she live with her parents?
   a) Because they looked after her children.   b) Because they only had two children.
3 Why did she travel by train?
   a) Because her parents needed her car.   b) Because she preferred it to going by car.
4 When would she be able to travel by car?
   a) When her children were old enough to go to school by bus.   b) When her children's school was able to buy a bus.
5 What did Freda's company do to encourage salespeople to sell a lot?
   a) They gave them a commission.   b) They paid their travel expenses.
6 Why did the living expenses she received not please Freda much?
   a) Because she hated being away from her family at night.
   b) Because the extra money was not enough for meals.
7 Did she think that everybody hated being away from their families at night?
   a) No, she did not.   b) Yes, she did.
8 Who was the manager of the company?
   a) Freda.   b) Helena Wright.
9 What was the amount of £203.22 for?
   a) It was Freda's hotel bill.   b) It was a mistake.
10 Had Freda bought any hotels in Manchester?
   a) No, she had not.   b) Yes, she had.

Exercise 2

Guided summary. Complete this story, using what you have read in the above story:

I work with Freda Livingstone.. Her job is to . . . and to try . . .. When she is away, she lives . . . and travels . . . because her car . . .. She not only gets a salary but also . . ., and while she is away on company business . . .. She hates . . . so . . ., but some other people . . .. Her manager once asked her about . . .. She asked her whether . . .. Freda told her that . . ., and the manager answered that . . ..

Exercise 3

> In conditional clauses referring to the past, the *had done* tense is used to show that the condition was not in fact fulfilled, and the *would have done* tense is used in the main clause (e.g. If Freda had not had any children, she would have used her car for travelling).
>
> In conditional clauses referring to the future, we can show that the condition is improbable by using the *did* tense. In the main clause we then have the *would do* tense (e.g. If Freda travelled in her car next week, her children would not be able to go to school).

Copy these sentences, putting each verb in brackets in the correct tense:

1 Freda (be) surprised if it (snow) in Manchester during her visit next June, because it has never snowed there in summer.
2 Freda (go) to Manchester in her own car last week if her parents (have) their own car.
3 She (go) to Manchester in her own car next week if her parents (buy) themselves a car, but they are too poor.
4 Freda (enjoy) her trip next week more if her children (go) with her, but they are still at school.
5 Perhaps Freda (have) a smaller hotel bill if she (not eat) so much.
6 Freda (spend) less in Manchester last time if she (go) to a cheaper hotel.

16

When I was a small boy in Greece and Turkey, I loved playing on old railway trucks at a part of the Hejaz railway which was no longer used. This is the railway that comes up from Arabia to the Sea of Marmara opposite Istanbul.

Then when I was sent to school in England, I used to travel by train from London to Salonica in Greece and back once a year for my summer holidays with my two younger brothers. We used to go third class, sitting on hard wooden seats for three days and three nights. Sleep was always a problem; when we nodded off, our heads dropped and we woke with a jump. We solved that problem by tying our scarves to the luggage rack above our heads and putting them under our chins. The only problem was that people coming into our compartment at stations used to think that we had hanged ourselves, having lost all hope of finishing our journey.

Once I got older, I found that I could do the journey by going through Germany, second class, in considerable comfort, having a sleeper at night only. At that time the Germans offered a sixty per cent discount on journeys through their country.

I used to love those journeys through beautiful scenery, without any worries or problems, changing trains in Munich and having a good lunch there one day, and then a real feast at Belgrade station the next evening, with plenty of time to enjoy it.

Since then I have done many journeys by car, ship and plane, but car journeys make me tired, and one has to put up with the often foolish and dangerous things that other drivers do; in a ship I sometimes get sick, and it is difficult to get away from the other passengers; and in a plane one sees nothing of the scenery, and passengers are pushed around like cattle at the airports.

No, give me the train, where I speed smoothly through beautiful country with no effort on my part; where I can go along and have an enjoyable meal in the dining car whenever I feel like it and without having to hurry, and where I can sleep like a baby in a comfortable bed while the train rushes on through the dark, whistling in a strangely sad and beautiful way, and bumping over points with a mysterious rhythm that I never seem to grow tired of.

Exercise 1

Look at these questions. Find the right answers. Then write the questions and the answers:

1 How did the writer of this story become interested in trains?
   a) He played on them.   b) He travelled on the Hejaz railway.
2 Why did it take three days and three nights for the writer to get home by train?
   a) Because his home was in England.   b) Because his home was in Greece.
3 When did he wake up with a jump?
   a) When his head dropped.   b) When people came into his compartment at stations.
4 How was his scarf useful?
   a) It prevented his head falling when he was asleep.
   b) It prevented his luggage falling off the rack.
5 How did he find he could travel more comfortably?
   a) By only having a sleeper at night.   b) By travelling through Germany.
6 Why was that cheaper?
   a) Because he got a sixty per cent discount.   b) Because he went second class.
7 Did he go the whole way in the same train?
   a) No, he did not.   b) Yes, he did.
8 Why are car journeys dangerous?
   a) Because of other drivers.   b) Because of the other passengers.
9 Does the writer of this story sleep well on trains?
   a) No, he does not.   b) Yes, he does.
10 What does he feel when the train bumps over points?
   a) He enjoys the rhythm.   b) He grows tired.

Exercise 2

In each of these (pairs of) sentences fill the empty space with a word that has the same root as the word *in italics*:

1   We call a person who *travels* a . . ..
2   We can say, 'Seats made of *wood* are hard' or '. . . seats are hard.'
3   I said, 'I have lost all *hope* of getting to Salonica this evening' and my brother answered, 'It's quite . . ., isn't it?'
4   In a railway station one can often see interesting *scenes* between travellers as they say goodbye to each other, and the beautiful . . . one sees from the window of one's train is just as interesting.
5   I don't get as *tired* in a train as I do in a car, and my brothers find it less . . . too.
6   One can say, 'Some drivers behave like *fools*' or 'Some drivers behave . . ..'
7   I sometimes feel *sick* on a ship, but my wife has never known what sea . . . means.
8   Many trains run very *smoothly*, and it is this . . . that makes them so comfortable.
9   We can say, 'Travel by train needs no *effort* on our part' or 'Travel by train is . . ..'
10 I said, 'The rhythm of the wheels going over points is full of *mystery* for me' and my brothers said, 'We find it very . . . too.'

Exercise 3

To show that two actions happen at the same time, we can use the -*ing* form of one of the verbs (e.g. 'The train rushes on through the dark, whistling in a strange and beautiful way' means 'The train rushes on through the dark and at the same time it whistles in a strange and beautiful way').

Join each pair of these sentences by replacing the part *in italics* with an -*ing* phrase:

1   I used to stand on a truck *and pretend it was moving.*
2   I used to travel from London *and take my younger brothers with me.*
3   Other passengers came into the compartment. *They were carrying a lot of luggage.*
4   I sat outside the station restaurant *and ate a big dinner.*
5   One can go along to the dining car and have a meal, *and take as much time as one wants.*

17

When Dave was sixty-five, he retired from his job in an office, and now he had to find ways of keeping himself busy and amused. He had always been interested in wild animals, so one day he decided to go to a safari park, where lions and leopards and other wild animals were not kept in cages, but in large open spaces, through which one drove in one's own car. It was round an old castle.

When his friend Joe, who was nearly seventy, heard that David planned to go to the safari park the following Saturday morning, he asked whether he could go with him, and Dave agreed happily, as he was often lonely, and did not much enjoy doing things by himself.

'We'll have to be careful not to get out of the car while we're in the park,' Joe said. 'Supposing a lion comes after us. Neither of us can run as fast as we used to!'

Dave laughed. They had both been good football players when they were young, and had played in the same team, winning a lot of matches together.

'How much do we have to pay to go into the safari park?' asked Joe.

'They charge five pounds each,' answered David, 'but if we show our pension cards, we'll be able to get in at half price.'

'Two pounds fifty?' said Joe. 'I don't think that's too bad.'

'Neither do I,' said Dave.

Joe earned a little money by doing a small part-time job in the evenings looking after an amusement arcade, and one of his jobs was to take the money out of the various games machines there, and take it to the bank. On that Friday evening he took a lot of small change from the machines, but as the bank was closed on Saturdays and Sundays he had to keep it at his house until the Monday.

That Saturday morning he had a good idea. 'I'll take as many of the coins as we need to the safari park and pay for our tickets with them,' he thought. 'That'll get rid of some of them.'

'I think that's a good idea,' he told Dave.

'So do I,' Dave answered.

The two men arrived at the safari park soon after nine o'clock in the morning and queued in Dave's old car to show their pension cards and buy their tickets. They could hear lions roaring inside the park.

When their turn came to pay, Joe put a big pile of small coins in front of the surprised ticket seller. 'There you are,' he said. 'That's five pounds.'

'Good heavens,' the ticket seller said, 'how long have you two poor old gentlemen been saving up to come to the safari park?'

Exercise 1

Look at these questions. Find the right answers. Then write the questions and the answers:

1   Why did Dave have to find ways of keeping himself busy and amused?
a) Because he had retired.   b) Because he was interested in wild animals.

2 How were the animals in the safari park kept?
a) In cages.   b) In open spaces.
3 How did one go round the park?
a) In one's car.   b) On foot.
4 Why was Dave happy when Joe wanted to go with him?
a) Because he preferred doing things with others.
b) Because they had played in the same team.
5 Why was it not wise to get out of Dave's car in the park?
a) Because they could not run faster than a lion.
b) Because they could not play football there.
6 Did everybody have to pay the same to go into the safari park?
a) No, they did not.   b) Yes, they did.
7 Where did Joe get a lot of coins one evening?
a) He collected them from machines in an amusement arcade.   b) He won them by playing games in an amusement arcade.
8 Why did he still have the coins on Saturday?
a) Because he wanted them for the safari park.
b) Because the bank was closed then.
9 How did the ticket seller know that they were retired?
a) Because they showed him their pension cards.
b) Because they looked like poor old gentlemen.
10 Had they been saving for a long time to come to the park?
a) No, they had not.   b) Yes, they had.

Exercise 2

Guided summary. Write a summary of the above story by answering these questions. Do not use numbers:

1 When did Dave retire? (*Dave . . .*)
2 Why did he decide to visit a safari park?
3 What did his friend Joe want to do? (*His friend Joe . . .*)
4 And why did Dave agree? (*and Dave . . .*)
5 How much did tickets cost?
6 But how could Dave and Joe get in at half price? (*but . . .*)
7 Where did Joe have a part-time job?
8 Why did he get a lot of coins one Friday evening?
9 Why could he not take them to the bank until Monday?
10 So what did he decide to do with some of them? (*so he . . .*)
11 What did the ticket seller think when he saw the coins?

Exercise 3

> If one wants to agree with what someone else has said, but one does not want to repeat her/his words, one can use *so*, to agree with an affirmative statement, or *neither/nor* to agree with a negative statement (e.g. 'I like safari parks.' 'So do I'; this means 'And I like safari parks too.' 'Dave hasn't got much money.' 'Neither/Nor has Joe'; this means 'And Joe hasn't got much money either'). Notice that after *so, neither* and *nor* in these cases, the verb comes before the subject (e.g. not 'So I do', but 'So do I').

Copy these sentences, but replace the parts *in italics* by a sentence with *neither, nor* or *so*:

1 Dave likes wild animals. *Joe likes wild animals too.*
2 Lions are dangerous animals. *Leopards are dangerous animals too.*
3 Joe can't run very fast now. *Dave can't run very fast now either.*
4 Dave had a pension card. *Joe had a pension card too.*
5 Pensioners do not pay the full price. *Children do not pay the full price either.*
6 Dave will not get out of the car in the safari park. *Joe will not get out of the car in the safari park either.*

Mr Jenkins had a sports car which he liked driving very fast. The problem was that there were speed limits on all the roads, but when he thought he could let the car go without being caught by the police, he did so.

Mrs Jenkins did not enjoy it when her husband drove very fast, especially as Mr Jenkins had had several accidents in his last car, in one of which Mrs Jenkins had had an arm broken. Mr Jenkins had also twice been caught speeding on a motorway, and he had had to go to court and pay a fine each time.

'Unless you're more careful,' his wife said, 'you'll lose your licence.'

One evening Mr and Mrs Jenkins were invited to a party at the house of some new friends. It was about forty kilometres from the Jenkins' home, and when Mr Jenkins looked on the map, he saw that there was a good main road most of the way, but not a motorway. 'That's good,' he thought. 'I can do it in twenty minutes if there are no police about.'

They started out, and Mr Jenkins drove along at his usual high speed, watching out for police cars in his mirror from time to time to make sure he was safe.

They reached their friends' house without any trouble and had a good time at the party. Then at half past ten, after dark, they began the return journey. Again Mr Jenkins drove very fast through the night, although it was raining.

'You'll have another accident unless you slow down,' his wife warned him, but he did not listen. Suddenly he heard a police siren just behind him, and the car following him turned on a blue light.

Mr Jenkins stopped at once and got out of his car angrily. 'Now look here, officer,' Mr Jenkins began at once, 'I've been keeping carefully just under seventy kilometres an hour. I'm sure of that because I've been looking at my speedometer every few seconds for the past twenty minutes.'

'Is that so, sir?' the policeman said, taking a book out of his pocket. 'Well, we didn't stop you for that. We stopped you to tell you that one of your rear lights isn't working. But if you were doing nearly seventy kilometres an hour, I'll have to give you a speeding ticket, because you're only allowed to do sixty along this road.'

Exercise 1

Look at these questions. Find the right answers. Then write the questions and the answers:

1 Why could Mr Jenkins not always drive as fast as he would like?
   a) Because he had a sports car.   b) Because of speed limits on all the roads.

2 Why did Mrs Jenkins think her husband might lose his licence?
   a) Because he had been caught speeding twice already.
   b) Because he had had several accidents.

3 At what speed did Mr Jenkins hope to drive to the new friends' house?
   a) 100 kilometres an hour.   b) 120 kilometres an hour.

4 Was he caught by the police on the way to the party?
   a) No, he was not.   b) Yes, he was.

5 Was it still light when they started home?
   a) No, it was not.   b) Yes, it was.

6 What other thing made driving difficult?
   a) A blue light.   b) Rain.

7 Why did Mr Jenkins think the police car had stopped him?
   a) For driving too fast.   b) For not driving carefully.

8 What had the police stopped him for?
   a) Because he was speeding.   b) To tell him that one of his lights was not working.

9 How did the police know this?
   a) Because it was dark.   b) Because they knew a lot about car lights.

10 Why did the policeman take a book out of his pocket?
   a) To find out what the speed limit was.   b) To write a speeding ticket for Mr Jenkins.

Exercise 2

In each of these (pairs of) sentences fill the empty space with a word that has the same root as the word *in italics*:

1 'Mr Jenkins has a very *fast* car.' 'Yes, it can go very . . ., can't it?'
2 'Has Mr Jenkins ever been stopped by the *police*?' 'Yes, a . . . stopped him only last week.'
3 Mr Jenkins *enjoys* driving fast, but his wife doesn't get much . . . out of it!
4 We can say, 'Drive with *care*' or 'Drive . . . .'
5 We can say, 'Mr Jenkins does not really *drive* sensibly' or 'Mr Jenkins is not really a sensible . . . .'
6 He likes *speed*, but that means that he is always in danger of getting a . . . ticket from the police.
7 His wife has *warned* him again and again, but he never listens to any of her . . . .
8 He thinks he is safer from the police when it is *dark*, but . . . is not always a protection.

Exercise 3

> We use *when* at the beginning of a clause which tells us something that we are sure will happen, and *if* at the beginning of a clause which tells us something that we are not sure will happen (e.g. We can say, 'It is going to rain, and Mr Jenkins will go home when it does' or 'Perhaps it will rain; Mr Jenkins will go home if it does'). *Unless* means 'if . . . not' (e.g. 'Mr Jenkins will not go home unless it rains').

Put *if, unless* or *when* in each space in these sentences:

1 Mr Jenkins will be caught speeding again . . . he is more careful.
2 He may lose his licence . . . he is caught again.
3 He always watches out for police cars . . . he is driving.
4 . . . Mr Jenkins had an accident last year, his wife had an arm broken.
5 . . . she had not been wearing a seat belt, she might have been killed.

19

Peter had always wanted a car, so as soon as he was old enough, he started to beg his mother to give him driving lessons. Usually children are very bad about learning from their parents, so they would rather be taught by someone else, but Peter's wages were not high enough to pay a driving instructor, so he was patient when his mother corrected him.

They went out in the evenings and at weekends, because Peter's mother had a job which kept her busy the rest of the time. After a time Peter passed his driving test, and his mother bought him a small secondhand car for his birthday. She made him pay for the licence, insurance, petrol and so on, because she said that would make him careful about driving economically.

'Insurance companies would rather not trust young drivers much,' she said to Peter laughingly, 'and as a matter of fact they're often right, so do drive carefully; and you'd better learn everything about your engine so that you can do something about it if necessary.'

Peter promised to do as his mother said. He used his car every day to drive to work and back, and he tried to be as careful as possible, but he did not learn much about the engine of the car, because he found it too difficult to understand the detailed instructions in the book he had.

Then one weekend he said to himself, 'I should be learning about the engine of my car, but I'd rather go for a drive in the country.' The sun was shining, it was spring, and the fields and woods were beautiful.

He was driving along quietly between green fields when suddenly a red light came on in the car and it slowly came to a stop. Peter tried to start it again, but in vain. He got out, opened the bonnet of the car and checked the petrol supply. It seemed all right.

Then suddenly he heard a cough very near his left ear. He turned and saw an old horse looking at him over the fence beside the road. 'You'd better have a look at the sparking plugs,' the horse said, and then went off to eat grass again.

Peter was so surprised that he ran to a farm a few hundred metres down the road, saw the farmer at the gate and told him what had happened.

'Was it an old horse with a white nose?' the farmer asked.

'Yes! Yes!' said Peter excitedly.

'Ah, well,' answered the farmer, 'you'd better not listen to him. He doesn't know much about cars.'

Exercise 1

Read these questions. Find the right answers. Then write the questions and the answers:

1 Why did Peter ask his mother to teach him to drive?
   a) Because he could not afford ordinary driving lessons.
   b) Because she was a patient teacher.
2 Did Peter buy a car when he passed his driving test?
   a) No, he did not.   b) Yes, he did.
3 Who paid for his licence and so on?
   a) Peter did.   b) Peter's mother did.
4 Which of the things that Peter promised his mother did he in fact do?
   a) He drove carefully.   b) He learnt everything about his car engine.
5 Were the instructions about the engine useful to him?
   a) No, they were not.   b) Yes, they were.
6 What did he do instead of studying the book?
   a) He learnt about the engine of his car.   b) He went for a drive in the country.
7 When the car slowly came to a stop, did Peter know how to start it again?
   a) No, he did not.   b) Yes, he did.
8 Who gave him advice about starting it?
   a) A farmer.   b) A horse.
9 Why did Peter not take this advice?
   a) Because he knew that it was wrong.   b) Because he was too surprised.
10 Who did not know much about cars?
   a) The farmer.   b) The horse.

Exercise 2

Guided summary. You have heard Peter's story, and you are telling it to your friends at work.

Say:
who taught Peter to drive a car.
why he did not have lessons from a driving instructor.
how he got his first car.
what he had to pay for.
what his mother suggested he should do, and why he did not
    do it.
what happened to the car while Peter was driving in the
    country one day.
what he did about it.
what he heard suddenly.
what had made this noise.
what it said.
what Peter did then.
what the farmer answered.

Exercise 3

> Instead of 'would prefer to do something' we can use
> 'would rather do something', and instead of 'it would be
> better if someone did something' or 'it would be advisable
> for someone to do something' we can use 'someone had
> better do something' (e.g. 'You'd/You had better go now.'
> 'No, I'd/I would rather stay a few more minutes').

Write these sentences, using rather or better:

1   Peter has a small secondhand car, but he would prefer to
    have a big new one.
2   He should learn about the engine of his car before it is too
    late.
3   He ought to drive carefully if he wants to avoid accidents.
4   He would prefer to drive fast, but he knows he ought not
    to.
5   The farmer told him that he should not listen to the old
    horse's advice.

A lot of people love the sea, and television has introduced us all to the beauties of life under water. But for most of us it is too expensive to buy or hire an aqualung, and also many of us are afraid to use one.

But anyone can learn to use a snorkel. You have a special mask to cover your eyes and nose, with glass or plastic in front to see through, and rubber round it to hold the mask tightly against your face to stop water getting in. The mask is fastened round the back of your head with one or two rubber straps, which can be made longer or shorter at the sides in order to fit your head comfortably.

Then you also have a curved tube, called a snorkel, one end of which you hold firmly between your teeth, while the other end sticks up out of the water in order to allow you to breathe.

While you are on the surface of the water, looking down at the fish and so on below, you can breathe comfortably, and then, when you want to dive, you stop breathing.

Of course, while you are diving, your snorkel fills with water, so when you come to the surface again, you blow out in order to empty the snorkel and be able to start breathing again.

The best place to use a snorkel if you are not a good swimmer and feel nervous when you are in deep water is on a reef, where you can put your foot down on the bottom when you feel tired or afraid.

The place I enjoyed most was on the south coast of Fiji, where I was working for a year. At low tide the outside edge of the reef was high, so that there was no fear of sharks coming in from the ocean, and because of its protection you could snorkel happily, floating easily and effortlessly over a large area of the most beautiful reef. There were fish of all colours, which were not afraid to come up quite close, sea anemones, beautiful seaweeds and everywhere clean white sand.

Among the rocks I would find big moray eels with fierce teeth and evil faces, hiding in small caves in order to shoot out and catch their prey. I did not dare to go near those, although I have seen divers on television making friends with them.

Some people go spearfishing with a snorkel, but I prefer to watch the beautiful creatures without trying to harm them.

Exercise 1

Look at these questions. Find the right answers. Then write the questions and the answers:

1 Why do most people not use an aqualung?
  a) Because they think it expensive and dangerous.
  b) Because they want to see all the beauties of life under water.

2 Why do you have to hold your mask tightly against your face?
  a) Because it covers your eyes and nose.   b) Because you use it under water.

3 How do you make the mask fit comfortably?
  a) By fastening it round the back of your head.   b) By tightening or loosening rubber straps.

4 Why is the snorkel tube curved?
  a) So that one end can go into your mouth.   b) So that water cannot get into it.

5 Can you breathe under water with a snorkel?
  a) No, you cannot.   b) Yes, you can.

6 How do you clear the water out of your snorkel?
  a) By blowing.   b) By coming to the surface again.

7 Why is a reef a good place for nervous swimmers?
  a) Because the water is deep there.   b) Because the water is shallow there.

8 What did you not have to be afraid of on the reef in Fiji?
  a) Fish of all colours.   b) Sharks.

9 Are moray eels sometimes friendly?
  a) No, they are not.   b) Yes, they are.

10 Can you use a snorkel when hunting fish?
  a) No, you cannot.   b) Yes, you can.

Exercise 2

In each of these (pairs of) sentences fill the empty space with a word that has the same root as the word *in italics*:

1 Life under water is *beautiful*, but one can only enjoy its various . . . by putting one's head under.
2 I said, 'I don't like having *tight* straps on my snorkel' and my wife answered, 'No, . . . at the back of one's head gives me a headache.'
3 One wants the mask to be *comfortable*. One does not want anything to interfere with one's . . . when one is diving.
4 You cannot *breathe* under water with a snorkel. You have to hold your . . . till you come up again.
5 You can say, 'I cannot *swim* well' or 'I am not a good . . . .'
6 If you are swimming with someone else, and you are *nervous*, your . . . often affects the other person too.
7 You can say, 'The reef *protected* me from sharks' or 'The reef was a . . . from sharks.'
8 You can say, 'I could float without *effort*' or 'I could float . . . .'
9 Moray eels look very *fierce*, but their . . . may only be to frighten other things.
10 People who *dive* are called . . ..

Exercise 3

One of the ways in which we can show purpose clearly is by using *in order to* + infinitive (e.g. 'Why did you buy a snorkel?' 'I bought it in order to see the beautiful fish on the reefs'). This is used in more formal English.

Copy these sentences, but use *in order to* to show purpose:

1 We use aqualungs so that we are able to stay under water for a long time, but we use snorkels so as to save money.
2 A snorkel has a curved tube so that it can be held in one's teeth at one end and at the same time stick up out of the water at the other.
3 You have to blow the water out of the tube to start breathing through it.
4 I went to Fiji for the purpose of working there.